THE KALUZA CONCEPT

SPECULATION ON THE NATURE OF REALITY

KEITH YOUNG

The Kaluza Concept.

I.S.B.N. No. 978-1-4092-7176-5

Contents.

Foreword.

Building on inspiration from cutting edge thinkers, "The Kaluza Concept" takes the reader beyond the edge of modern science and into a higher dimensional realm where consciousness dictates its own destiny through the creation of multiple realities and a process of self-refinement, eventually achieving supreme omniscience.

This book proposes a meaning and significance to all we experience as physical beings.

I can pretty much guarantee that you have never read a book quite like this one! It makes a brazen attempt to bring under one tidy umbrella such inexplicable and disparate phenomena as ghosts and poltergeists, precognition, timeslips, déjà vu, appearances and disappearances, experience of alternative realities, dowsing and, to top it all, life after death!

All of the books I have managed to get hold of on subjects such as this have left me with a vague feeling of "unfinished business" at the end, a feeling that they could have gone further with their work and increased its scope.

I hope the resulting book makes a good attempt to take that further step and increase that scope.

The ultimate goal of this work is to postulate a structure for reality which not only allows for, but actually requires, the survival of consciousness after death. Without the latter, the whole scheme of things would seem pointless!

For this reason alone, I would suppose that this book applies to everyone on the planet, as we all have a vested interest here!

But a lot of people tend to discard ideas such as those contained here as futile, theosophical ramblings with no scientific reference whatsoever by some sad and lonely maniac with only a cat for a friend.

To address such issues, all the ideas in this book are built on some scientific foundation, from relativity to psychology and M-Theory to quantum physics – they are just taken that little bit further, the imagination is stretched!

So, I won't prattle on any further, but do read on. Perhaps these ideas have been expressed elsewhere that I'm unaware of, but if the reader finds them innovative or even thought-provoking, then I've achieved my second objective.

The first one was to stop them from "bugging" me!!! Now, perhaps I can relax and listen to guitar bands again!

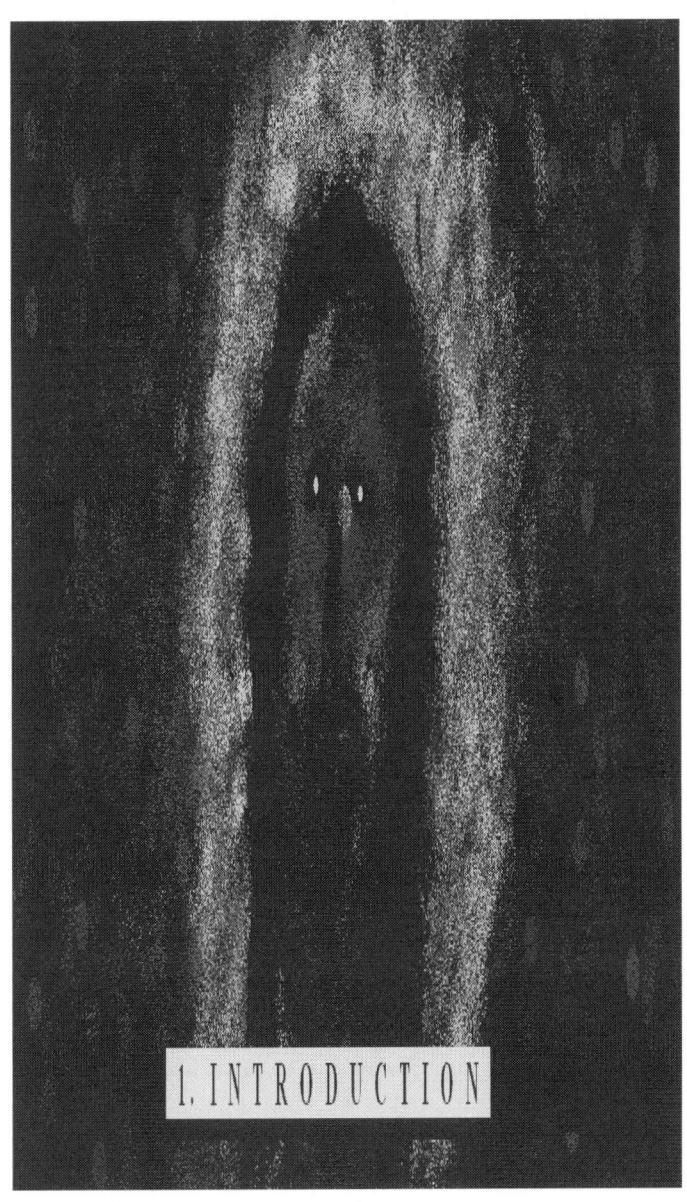

1. INTRODUCTION

1 . Introduction.

Just what is the nature of reality? Let's face it, we take reality pretty much for granted. It's the world around us, the world of technology, the world of big business, cities, housing estates, possessions, money to finance these things. This is the superficial reality created by the human mind, a superficial reality which is beginning to have a serious effect on our home planet, as our elected world leaders are beginning – perhaps too late – to realise.

In our contemplative moments, we may gaze into the night sky and see the myriads of stars deep in space, catch a glimpse even of other galaxies, perhaps like our own, and wonder at their beauty and deep mystery, mysterious only because our technology has not reached a stage where we can explore these distant recesses directly.

Our scientists have made great inroads on the mysteries of the universe, estimating distances of stars, speculating on planets orbiting them, and also on the possibility of other sentient beings like ourselves.

The greatest human minds have woven elaborate theories explaining, to the best of our ability, the laws of gravity, the structure of space-time, the behaviour of the minutest particles of which we can conceive, placing us comfortably at the intellectual centre of our universe, and putting us on a firm, deterministic footing with which we challenge nature and its former mysteries.

Indeed, our knowledge seems to strengthen and add consistency and solid foundation to an external reality which can apparently never be questioned. We go about our everyday existence, working, taking holidays, raising our families, buying and improving our homes, acquiring our possessions to give "meaning" and "value" to our lives, safe in the knowledge that the Druids of our day, the scientists, have all the big questions safely in hand.

But every day, evidence comes to light, be it by personal experience or media exposure of someone else's experience, of a disquieting event which seems to tear the very fabric of our beliefs. These events are usually blanked out by the mind as being hallucinatory in nature, or if they are reported by the media, are covered in a very brief and understated way, usually subsidiary to the political events of the day, in the spirit of a curiosity.

Documentaries are often made of the more persistent strange events, such as the Bermuda Triangle, and people watch and wonder, but tend to dismiss it as no more than an interesting sideshow, outside the province of the all-important, all-embracing scientific standpoint of the day.

This attitude is a "cop out" from any attempt to explain these events in scientific terms. The paranormal is therefore usually put firmly on the back burner as a side issue which can be dabbled in by fringe scientists and crackpots but left well alone by serious researchers and level headed members of the lay public.

In my opinion, this is a habit which must be broken, as events which are currently termed "paranormal" will eventually find their way under the umbrella of the "serious" scientific mainstream, as the latter progresses toward a fuller understanding of the true nature of reality.

But without further pontificating on the injustices of our current world paradigm, let's have a brief look at some typical examples of unexplained phenomena which may give you the general gist of the panoply of incidents which current scientific thought fails to embrace. The readers who wish to get to the "nitty gritty" of the text, and who are already well informed on incidents of the unexplained, can quite easily skip the following section if a feeling of déjà vu descends!! As a result, these examples will be covered only briefly, as books devoted to these subjects are many, and in depth repetition of their content would be futile here, but I feel a brief mention would be worthwhile to place them in the context of the ideas I intend to expound in these pages.

Stories abound of strange disappearances. Children going missing, the search parties for which produced no results whatsoever, only for the children to be found several days later, having no idea that they had been missing!

They appear to have entered some kind of time lapse, where time for them bore little relation to the time experienced by those uninvolved.

As the children could not be found by an extensive search, it also suggests that not only time, but space, was involved, linking these two concepts inextricably together.

Even more strange stories abound of people simply disappearing instantaneously never to be seen again by anyone whatsoever!

No explanation, no warning, no particular noted strange behaviour beforehand; an instantaneous vanishing!

It makes you wonder how many unreported cases occur where there were no witnesses to report the baffling phenomena, or witnesses were simply so baffled that their minds ignored the evidence of their own eyes!

Furthermore, poltergeist phenomena, which can cause water to spill out of sealed pipes, and can throw objects out of locked rooms through solid walls or doors, also seem to defy our solid, deterministic view of reality, the existence of another dimension beyond our usual three being a sensible postulate to explain these occurrences.

The cases so far seem to challenge our view of reality as a concrete structure itself, but what about the immutability of space and time? Space is essential to our view of reality as regards the distance and relationship to each other of objects therein – essential in essence to our logical comprehension of our physical location in relation to the world, and indeed the whole universe, around us. Our conception of space ensures that we perceive that all objects are not in the same place at once.

Time, too, or at least our sensation of this, is essential to our functioning on a physical level with our reality. Cause precedes effect in a "logical" fashion which enables us to predict and interact with our environment in a "sensible" manner, without which our physical existence would cease to have meaning. Time, in effect, prevents all events from happening at once.

But there are certain documented experiences which seem to attack these two cornerstones of our deterministic view of reality.

There is a story, from way back in the late sixteenth century, of a soldier who seemed greatly out of place in the location in question.

Obviously arousing some suspicion in his would be colleagues, the anomalous chap was questioned and replied that he was ordered to guard a residence which turned out to be thousands of miles away from the location in question (bear in mind that this was the sixteenth century, way before supersonic jet propulsion methods had been even thought about!).

Furthermore, he recited details about an event which had occurred in this distant location the night before which obviously in that day and age could not be immediately corroborated.

However, corroboration of his story came about two months later by conventional means (namely, a ship)...all the timings were absolutely spot on. Only the soldier's transportation was anomalous!

There are also numerous reported cases of people having either a vague inkling through dreams, or a more pronounced idea, of what is going to happen in the future, either by vivid pre-enactment of the event in the dream state, or a more symbolic pre-enactment open to interpretation after the event.

There are also many accounts of "time-slips", or "retro-cognition", whereby certain people have seemingly instantaneously travelled back in time and witnessed events – and even interacted with people – from long ago.

Such accounts seem to challenge our stance on time as immutable. Perhaps only on the level of our perceptions, it is.

The latter two examples in particular seem to invoke the action of our own consciousness as an active participant in the sensations of these vagaries of our "deterministic" reality.

Indeed, there does seem to be extensive evidence from numerous sources, respected scientists with an open mind and an innate sense of curiosity, plus what most would term level-headed, down to earth people, that consciousness is a lot more complex than we would initially believe.

Specially gifted people do seem to be able to perform mental acts which most of us could only dream about, and therefore usually dismiss as "a load of old bull", to use a popular colloquialism.

There was a story of such a gifted old woman, who people "naturally" dismissed as a "witch", who, at will, could leave her physical body and wander wherever she fancied as a free entity.

This is the phenomenon known as astral projection, which certain people have honed to a "fine art", but which is something that we all perform to a greater or lesser extent involuntarily in an unconscious state.

However, highly gifted people can wander around in the astral as easily as the majority of us walk around in the physical, and even later report accurately events they have witnessed whilst in that state!

Now, certain people are termed "sensitives" i.e. they are especially perceptive to impressions left in an environment of which most of us are unaware.

These people pick up on impressions left in a certain place where, for instance, there has been a tragic, traumatic event.

But how on earth could they do this if some consciousness, at some point in time, had not left that impression there in the first place?

Does this not strongly suggest an interaction of consciousness with what we normally term the external, physical environment, suggesting a certain melding of the two normally disparate concepts?

Particularly interesting are investigations into dowsing . This is the process whereby a pendulum is held over different materials and it can usually be found that the pendulum reacts at different discrete lengths of string for different material. Even more baffling, from an orthodox point of view, is that even abstract concepts such as life and death, if visualised in the mind's eye, have a reaction at a certain string length. How on earth could this be? How can an abstractly visualised concept invoke a reaction in a thoroughly materialistic pendulum, unless we involve some kind of fusion of consciousness and matter? Furthermore, reactions seem to reach a limit at a certain length of string, and then as the string is lengthened further, the same sequence of reactions is repeated, which seems to hint at the nature of a wavelength, even for objects and abstract concepts.

At first sight, this would seem to form a link with the views of quantum mechanics, with its associated wave-particle duality. In fact, de Broglie suggested that even macroscopic objects such as those tested by dowsing – abstract concepts aside – would be imbued with a wavelength. Perhaps this is the sum of all the wavelengths of constituent particles, an interesting idea which will be pursued later within these pages.

Before we reluctantly leave this fascinating – if unorthodox – subject, I would just like to mention the abstract notion we regard as "time".

When time is tested with a pendulum, it is apparently found that a reaction for time is initiated at length 60", and one particular investigator in this field made the strange observation that time appears to be static.

He came to this conclusion on the basis that the pendulum gives different reactions for things that are static and things that are dynamic.

This links in with interesting ideas put forth by the Russian philosopher P.D. Ouspensky on time as another spatial dimension only incompletely perceived by our consciousness as motion.

"It is necessary to admit that by one term, "time", we designate really two ideas – "a certain space" and "motion upon that space". This motion does not exist in reality, and it seems to us as existing only because we are looking at the world as if through a narrow slit, and are seeing the lines of intersection of the time plane with our three dimensional space only."

Going back to the idea of consciousness interacting with external reality, it has also been suggested that sightings of, for instance, the Loch Ness monster and various other aquatic creatures of indeterminate species could actually be some kind of ghost, not necessarily a supernatural spirit.

In fact, C.G. Jung, one of the most eminent psychologists of our time, suggested that U.F.O.s could be projections of some deep unconscious need in mankind on the outside world.

This is a particularly interesting corroboration of the point I'm developing by an eminent scientist who came up with groundbreaking ideas in the field of psychology.

If an apparent physical, external object could be a projection of the unconscious mind, what else in the "external" world is of a similar nature?

By definition, if it's unconscious, we're hardly likely to be aware of it in the normal sense, but it nevertheless suggests a melding of mind and matter.

Interesting points crop up here:

1. Do these phenomena represent the impingement of other realities on our own?
2. Are they projections of the combined unconscious minds of our species?
3. Are our unconscious minds instigating a kind of "phase shift" of realities bringing glimpses of alternative realities into our own?

It has been suggested it might be possible to construct a machine to gain access to these other levels of reality. Such a machine "would necessitate some kind of dynamo to produce a field of force around the experimenters"

It is interesting to note that stories of the Philadelphia Experiment, wherein a U.S. Navy ship, the U.S.S. Eldridge, was allegedly caused to disappear and reappear instantaneously at some distant location, involve the use of an electro-magnetic field of extraordinary power.

One wonders if the use of strong electromagnetic fields causes a phase shift of the wavelength of reality introducing other possible realities into our own. Strong electromagnetic fluctuations often accompany paranormal events.

For instance, there are many records dating back centuries of what we would term anomalous occurrences accompanying particularly violent electromagnetic storms (that's thunderstorms to you and me!), including sightings of strange and "terrifying" (to the medieval mind) creatures and evidence, in the aftermath of the storms, of unidentifiable footprints and so forth.

Perhaps the strong electromagnetic fields created a temporary bridge between alternative realities caused by some kind of phase shift.

So, what have we so far? Our picture of a "solid" reality certainly seems on shaky ground!

People mysteriously disappearing, people transported apparently instantaneously to distant locations, the ability of "seers" to view events yet to come to pass, time slips, or retro-cognition, where people have witnessed events long past, or seen places as they were long ago. Also, the apparent ability of certain people to travel outside the confines of their physical bodies, sense impressions left upon the environment by people suffering great emotion – be it positive or negative – plus the hint by dowsing, a discipline thousands of years old, that matter could be represented by a waveform, providing a link with quantum physics.

Add to this the apparent incursion into our reality of other planes of existence not normally detected by ourselves, and apparently facilitated by strong electromagnetic fields, and we realise that our conventional view of the world is woefully inadequate in terms of contemporary science.

But we are all conscious beings, and considering this, what role does our consciousness play in all this, and is it possible that the facet of ourselves of which we are aware in everyday terms is but one of an infinite number of pan-dimensional manifestations of consciousness which transcend the whole structure of reality itself?

The big question is:

Have we any evidence of this? Is there any anecdotal or scientific evidence that our consciousness can transcend the limitations of the physical brain and the confines of our three dimensional "prison"?

At this juncture, I would like to have a brief look at N.D.E.s, or Near Death Experiences, to push us a little further into the investigation of the teetering parapet we term "the real world".

So, what exactly is an N.D.E.? Well, more accounts of these occur since medical advances have been achieved which result in more people who would previously have died being resuscitated. They, in effect, live to tell the tale! And a fascinating tale it is!

To begin with, common experiences seem to cross the gulf between nationalities, age, religious beliefs, personality, plus a whole host of other differences between people who undergo this experience. This seems to lend an objective aspect to the phenomenon which suggests these people all go to the same place.

The first stage consists of awareness of no longer being in the physical body whilst still retaining sentience and a sense of self. This part is usually confusing and the entity may still try to attract the attention of the living. At this point, an increased sense of self identity is experienced. An acute sense of freedom is experienced too, like breaking out of a cage, and at this point, fear turns to blissful understanding (or perhaps remembering?) and a real sense of peace.

There is also a sense of still being in some type of body, albeit very unlike the physical one. Some people describe it as a mixture of colours, or an energy field. Some people say they appear to be composed of light with a barely perceptible structure of some kind.

So, a conscious energy field would seem to be suggested here. Max Planck, the renowned physicist, said:

"Energy is the origin of all matter. Reality, true existence, is not matter, which is visible and perishable, but the invisible, immortal energy – that is truth."

There is then a sense of going through some sort of a passageway towards an intense light. This passageway can be described as a tunnel or a dark space with a bright light at the end. Others experience this transition as passing through an elaborate doorway or climbing a vast stairway.

Either way, the sense of entering another realm is experienced – the mode of entry is probably due to personal conceptualisation.

Once in the light, they are greeted by beautiful and intensely luminescent entities filled with what experiencers describe as "love".

According to form, there occurs a blurring of concepts here: light becomes love becomes light!

This light is described as being much brighter – more energetic – than anything we experience in our universe, and yet it is warm, vibrant and alive, not unpleasant in any way. In this sense, one could interpret the light as being conscious.

N.D.E.ers frequently meet up with friends and relatives who have died, all bathed in the same luminescence. Pastoral scenes are often described, and even luminescent cities that defy earthly description. As light is electromagnetic energy, could this all be a vast energy field in which consciousness is distinctly manifest individually and yet is absorbed by the whole?

A being radiating total love and understanding then takes them on a life review, which has been described as a full colour, three dimensional panoramic view of every single action performed in the physical life, but from a third person perspective and not in time as we experience it normally. Every event seems to be there at once, but yet each is experienced individually, complete with the effects – positive or negative – on the recipients of the person's actions. It appears the person is able to enter the consciousness of the recipient of the action – out of time as we know it – and therefore experience at first hand the consequences of their own actions.

Many people come away from this review with the feeling that the most important thing in life is love, and the second, acquisition of knowledge. These two attributes apparently transcend "death" with us.

People who have undergone N.D.E.s say that time is greatly compressed, as if it has no logical meaning. A description of time in this realm, wherever it is, is totally meaningless: seconds, minutes, hours, days, months, years, centuries are all the same! So much for the immutability of time!

This brings to mind again comments on page 15 by the Russian philosopher P.D. Ouspensky relating to time as a spatial dimension perceived incompletely on the physical plane as motion.

"If we imagine a receptivity which is on a higher level than our consciousness, possessing a broader angle of view, then this receptivity will be able to grasp, as something simultaneous, all that is happening for us during a certain length of time – minutes, hours, a day, a month. Within the limits of its moment, such a receptivity will not be in a position to discriminate between before, now, after; all this will be, for it, now. 'Now' will expand."

Normal spatial boundaries are also apparently transcended in N.D.E.s. If entities want to go somewhere, they simply *are* there with no more than a passing thought.

So, the consciousness we are aware of with our everyday lives appears to have stranger attributes than we could ever have imagined.

If our consciousness, released from its physical confines, is so powerful, is it so surprising that it can affect, and even be a part of, the physical events in the world around us, whether we are aware of it or not? But what are "we"?

In the pages that follow, I will attempt to give my views on what "we" are, why "we" are here, and the possible mechanism by which "we" can fulfil our eventual destiny in total unity.

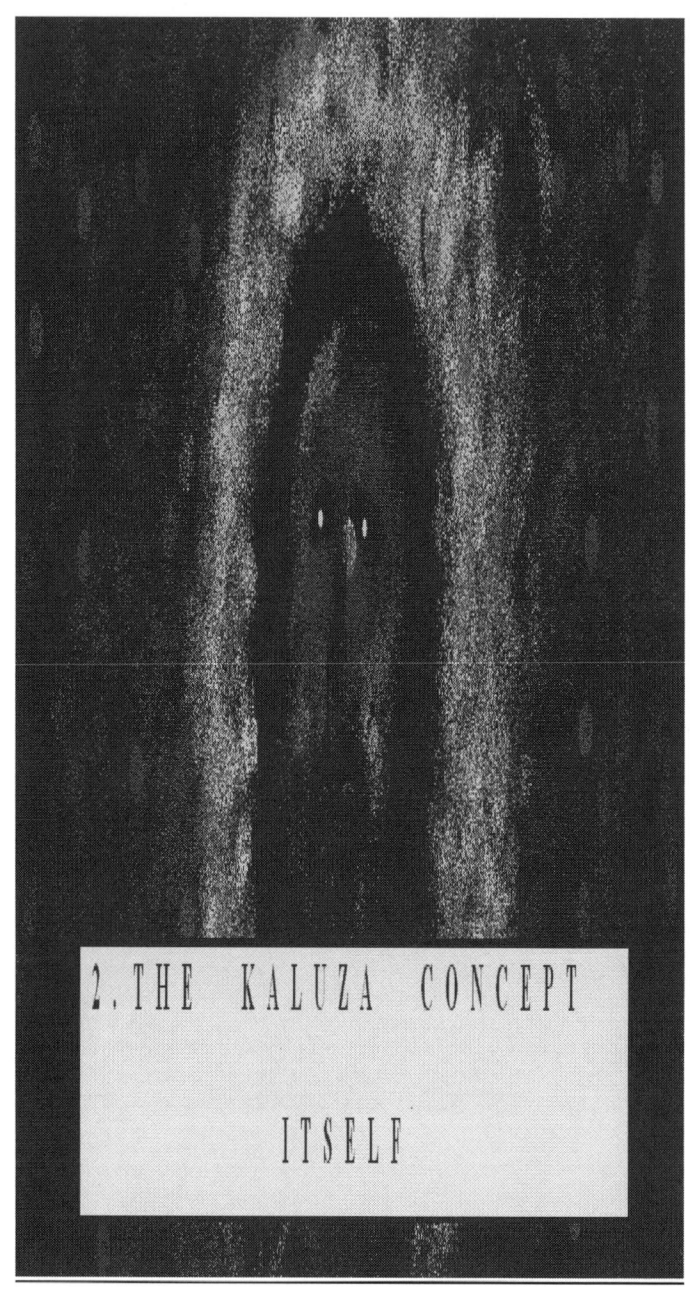

2.THE KALUZA CONCEPT

ITSELF

2. The Kaluza Concept Itself.

So, we seem to have some inkling that consciousness can function independently of the physical brain, and not only this, it seems to "go" somewhere else, a seemingly magical place full of love and harmony, where pure thought would seem to be the order of the day, and released from physical constraints, anything is possible.

The year: 1919. The man: a little known Polish mathematician named Theodor Kaluza. The place: the University of Konigsberg.

Kaluza suggested that the universe may possess more than the three dimensions than meet the physical eye. We simply cannot perceive them.

As an analogy, I intend to adapt an idea prevalent at the moment in modern physics.

This analogy consists of a thin tube inside, say, a thermometer. Now, from a distance, the tube would seem to be a one dimensional object; i.e. movement could only occur from left to right or vice versa, along its length. But upon closer inspection, the tube actually possesses a thickness, a second dimension, one that is in the shape of a circle and is curled around it.

See Figs. 1 and 2 overleaf.

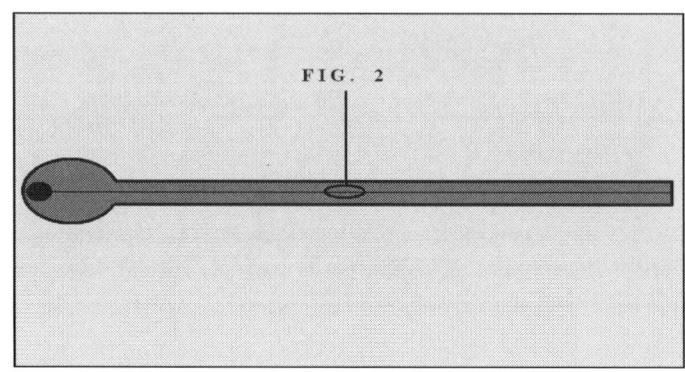

Fig. 1. From a Distance, the Tube Appears One Dimensional.

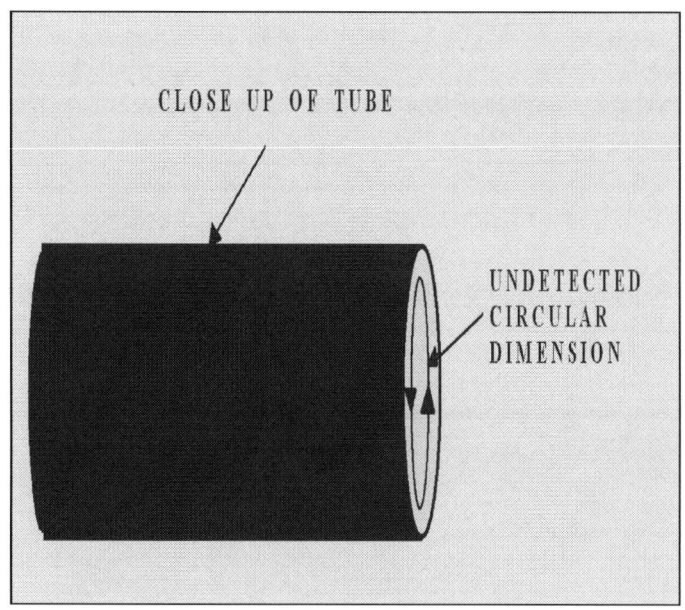

Fig. 2. Upon Closer Inspection, a Further Circular Dimension Appears.

26

Thus, an object within the tube can be located using two pieces of data: its distance from the left or the right hand side of the tube's end, and its position around the inner girth.

In the same way, Kaluza suggested that every point in our three dimensional space contains tiny curled up dimensions which are far too small for us to detect.

Below, I have included a two dimensional representation of the extended three dimensions of common experience with the extra dimensions shown as circles at each intersection. (See Fig.3.)

So, just how small is this extra dimension? In 1926, the Swedish mathematician Oskar Klein combined Kaluza's initial suggestion with ideas from the emerging field of quantum mechanics, and came up with a suggestion that the additional circular dimension may be as small as the Planck length: 10 to the power of minus 35 metres.

The extra dimensional theory became known as Kaluza-Klein Theory.

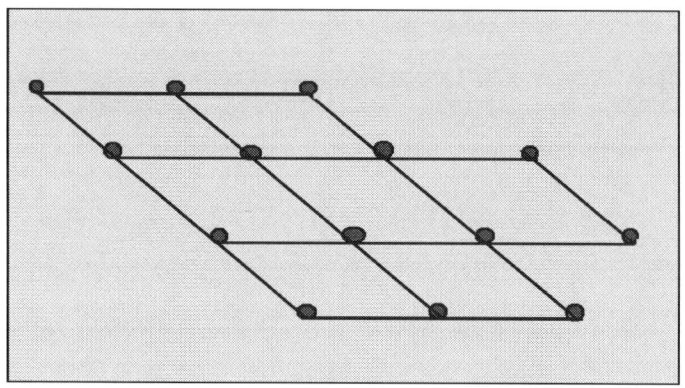

Fig.3. Curled Up Dimensions.

Unfortunately, at the time of its initial suggestion, quantum mechanics and quantum field theory burst onto the scene, and the extra dimensional idea was put firmly on the back burner.

Once quantum theory was reasonably firmly established, more research into extra dimensions was undertaken, elaborating further on Kaluza's original proposal by adding more curled up dimensions.

But in 1984, String Theory entered the fray. So, what is String Theory?

Well, briefly stated, physicists have been searching for decades for a theory which would unite quantum mechanics and general relativity, bringing into the same fold the strong and weak nuclear forces, electromagnetism and gravity – the unified field theory.

General relativity works really well on the macroscopic scale of galaxies, stars and planets, but tends to break down when the frantic undulations of the "quantum foam" are encountered. This is where quantum mechanics tends to take over, from the smooth geometrical space-time sweep of general relativity.

Now, the standard model of quantum mechanics is based on the idea that the elementary building blocks of all matter are actually point particles, which basically have zero size and are capable of probing the sub-Planck length scales where quantum fluctuations become so troublesome.

String theory replaces these point particles with tiny one-dimensional oscillating loops called "strings".

As these are of an extended nature, albeit vanishingly small, they smear out the inconvenient quantum undulations at the sub-Planck scale previously causing the rift between general relativity and quantum mechanics.

Furthermore, the mass and the force charges of the elementary particles, previously unexplained, are said in string theory to be produced as a result of the particular oscillations of the loops of which they are made, rather like the oscillation of a guitar string produces a particular note.

Thus, rather than being disparate phenomena, all the basic ingredients from which the universe is made are brought under one umbrella, and are accounted for by string vibrations.

Thus, a cosmic symphony exists!

But initially, this cosmic symphony was rather cramped in style by being limited merely to the three dimensions with which we are familiar – the resonance chamber was too small! The mathematics simply didn't add up and yielded negative probabilities outside the acceptable range.

But, calculations showed that if the strings were allowed to oscillate in nine independent spatial directions, the equations worked out.

Thus, Kaluza-Klein theory was resurrected, with six curled up spatial dimensions at every point in three dimensional space, instead of the initial one. String theory, a strong contender for the "theory of everything", demanded this.

A particular class of six-dimensional geometrical shapes satisfy the equations of string theory, and these are known as Calabi-Yau spaces, in honour of two mathematicians, Eugenio Calabi, from the University of Pennsylvania, and Shing-Tung Yau, from Harvard University.

One example is shown (albeit two dimensionally!) in Fig. 4 overleaf.

This amazingly complex looking shape should now be interchanged with the circles originally proposed by Kaluza as shown in Fig. 3.

Thus we see that every single point in our three dimensional space is punctuated by one of these amazingly intricate spaces. One sweep of the hand circumnavigates countless Calabi-Yau

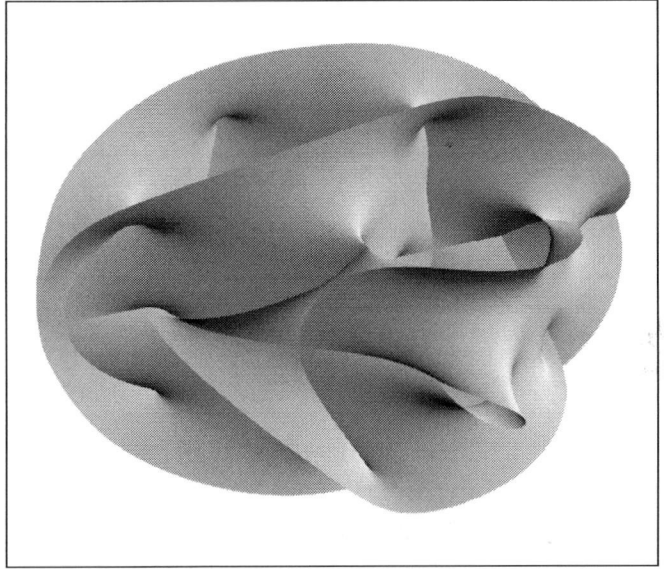

Fig.4. A Six-Dimensional Calabi-Yau Manifold.

spaces (or manifolds) an enormous number of times, repeatedly returning to the starting point.

One is reminded of one of those old-fashioned panes of glass dented with numerous circles, each of which captures your movement in an exaggerated fashion.

Now, so far each Calabi-Yau space is regarded as a separate entity, rather like an isolated pixel on a computer monitor. But it seems to me rather uncharacteristically wasteful of nature to use six whole dimensions "merely" as a resonance chamber for string vibrations, even though these do determine the most fundamental characteristics of the universe as we know it!

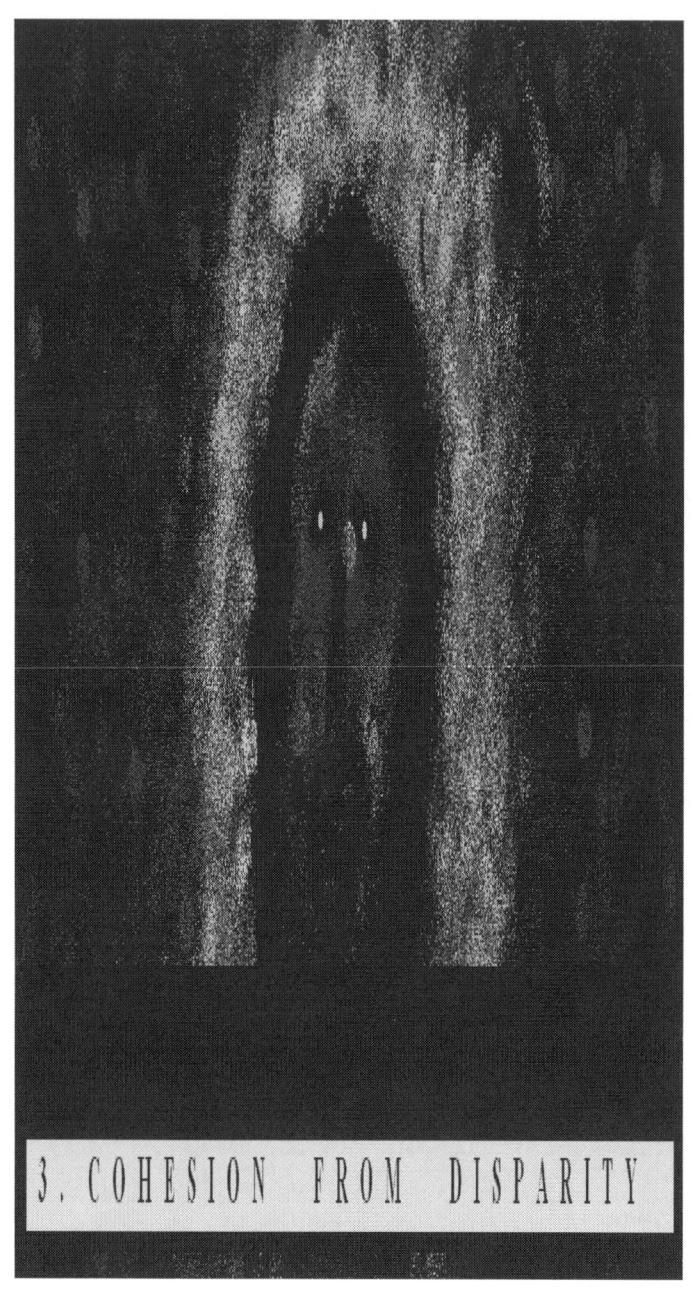

3. COHESION FROM DISPARITY

3. Cohesion From Disparity.

I ask you to bear with me as we make the first leap of the imagination.

I have already mentioned the idea that each Calabi-Yau space can be thought of as a single pixel on a computer monitor. When you look closely at the screen – not to be recommended on a regular basis! – and focus on an individual pixel, it is meaningless in isolation.

But as you change your perspective and focus outwards to bring in more pixels, an image begins to form until, when you take in the screen as a whole, a coherent picture is perceived.

In the same way, an isolated Calabi-Yau space is merely a six-dimensional arena in which strings can oscillate, but a change of perspective bringing all the Calabi-Yau spaces into play together would, in my opinion, form a coherent six-dimensional higher space.

At this point, permit me to indulge in another rough analogy!

Imagine the chapter art assembled from separate squares but forming a coherent whole.

If I were then to do the art world a favour and roll each one of these squares into a tight cylinder, there would be no hint of the resplendent beauty (!) which lies within, but merely, from a distance, one-dimensional strips.

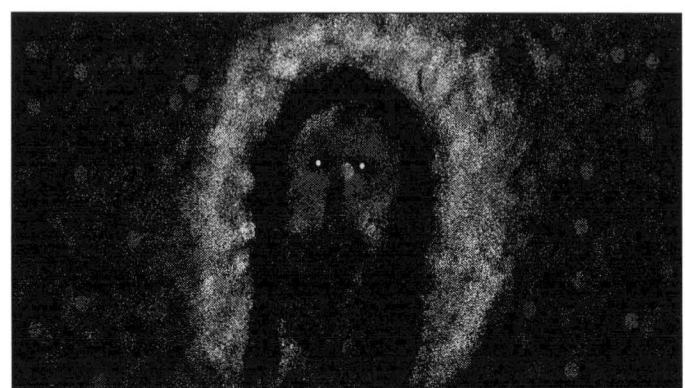

Fig.5. The Chapter Art.

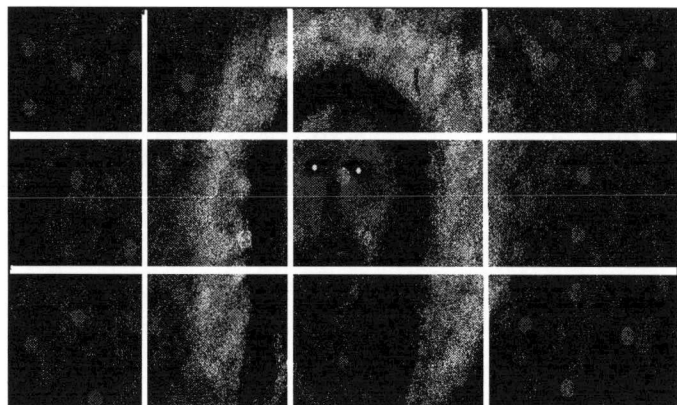

Fig 6. The Chapter Art in Sections.

The lower section of Fig.6 represents the way we perceive the Calabi-Yau spaces from our three-dimensional, physical perspective.

But if you imagine that at every point in our three-dimensional space, a Calabi-Yau manifold resides, then a "chunk" of space-time would actually appear as in Fig.7 below, which is a matrix consisting of Calabi-Yau spaces, one of which is represented in Fig.4.

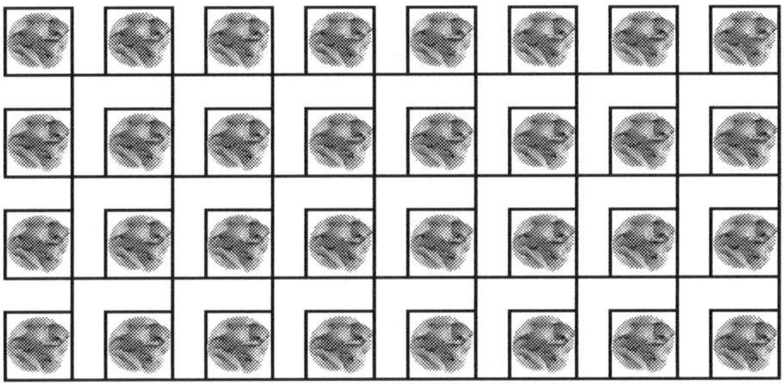

Fig.7. A Very Schematic View of Space-time With a Calabi-Yau Space at Every Intersection.

If this change of perspective is employed, then the six-dimensional higher space seems to dominate the picture, relegating our familiar extended three dimensions to mere points of intersection between the six-dimensional spaces. Reality appears to be viewed almost from an "inside out" perspective.

Now for the second leap of imagination! How is this change of perspective achieved? It certainly seems to be different on a mundane, everyday level. Barring leaps of the imagination such as the one just taken,that appears to be all they are – leaps of imagination.

But recall I mentioned earlier that consciousness, when released from the physical brain, in quite a few documented cases, appears to "go somewhere else". Where is this "somewhere else"? Well, you may have already pre-empted my suggestion of the six-dimensional higher space. Where else?

While you're digesting this outrageous suggestion, this seems a good point to indulge in a brief digression into the realm of string theory.

Further investigation into the nature of strings has revealed what physicists construe to be further dimensions closely associated with the strings themselves.

A one-dimensional oscillating loop is known as a "string", or "one-brane". Inference of a two-dimensional structure to the string itself (recall the garden hose analogy) transforms the string into a "two-brane". Mathematical inference has increased the dimensionality of the previously fundamental string, or "one-brane", up to and including a "nine-brane", i.e. a nine-dimensional membrane. This is why the theory is coming to be known as "membrane", rather than "string", theory.

However, I believe these are not additional dimensions as such, but a revelation of the true structure of strings through all nine existing spatial dimensions – three extended, physical dimensions and six higher Calabi-Yau dimensions.

In this way, as Ouspensky speculates, our physical reality is a cross-section of a higher dimensional reality.

After that digression, at this juncture, I wish to speculate upon the nature of consciousness itself, hopefully casting doubt upon the traditional point of view regarding this "sacred cow" as well!

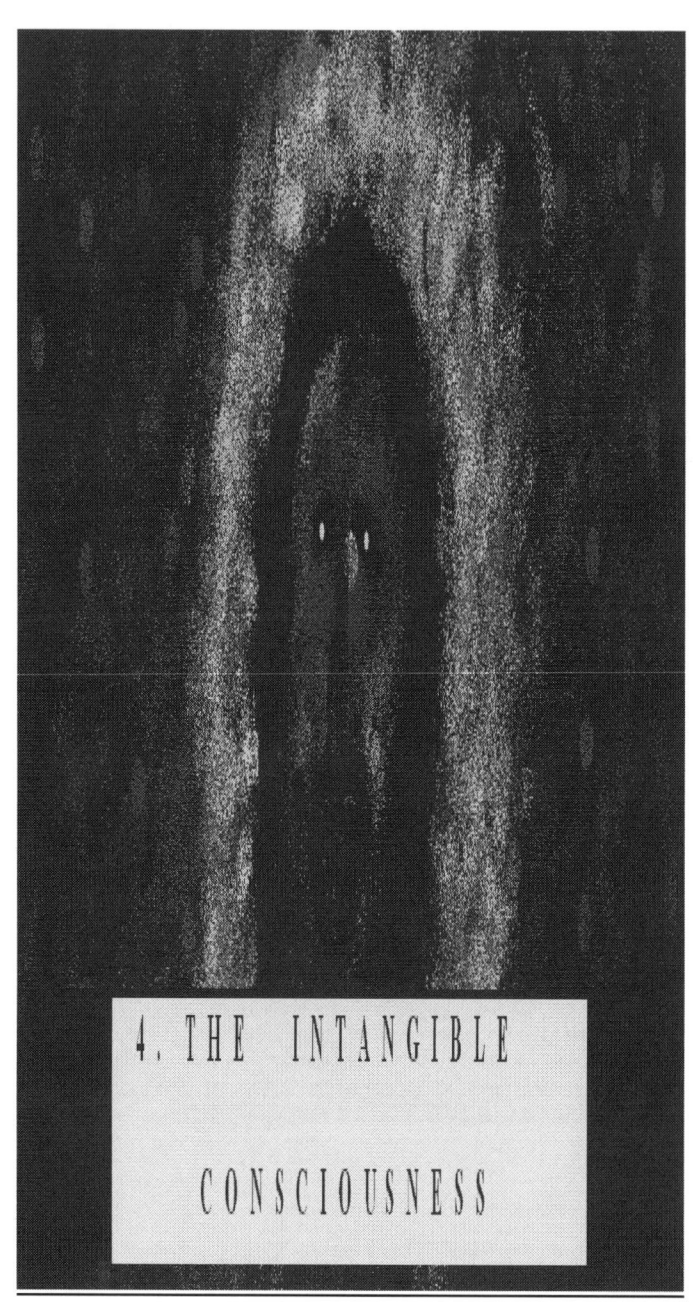

4. THE INTANGIBLE

CONSCIOUSNESS

4. The Intangible Consciousness.

Consciousness, despite being the most personal experience possible, is perhaps the most elusive phenomenon in terms of exploring its nature.

Attempts have been made to explain its existence in terms of the non-local quantum correlations which can occur over widely separated distances. In a nutshell, this is where two formerly linked quantum particles can still display correlative behaviour even when separated by light years of space – too large a distance for information to pass instantaneously without exceeding the speed of light. I wish to elaborate further on this later in the text in relation to alternative realities.

The background state of consciousness is what physicists call a "steady state", uniform in space and persistent in time. This settled uniformity is rare in dynamic processes, but it does occur in materials in "condensed phases", such as magnets, super-fluids, super-conductors, laser light, electric currents in metals and sound waves in crystals. These all display coherence, such that the atoms or molecules behave as one.

So how does this relate to the brain? Super-fluids and superconductors only exist at very low temperatures, whereas the brain is obviously at body temperature. So what condensed phase operates at this temperature?

Enter Herbert Frohlich of Liverpool University who is the source of the idea that quantum coherent waves could be generated in the neural network. He viewed the electric potential across the neuron membrane as the observable feature of some form of underlying quantum order. He claimed to show that with an oscillating charge in a thermal bath, large numbers of quanta may condense into a coherent state called a Bose Condensate.

For consciousness to attain the holism that it does, a similar state would appear to be necessary. So, how does this happen? What is the mechanism?

Now, I have a view on this which is unconventional to say the least, and if I inserted it at this point, out of context of my later arguments, it would be virtually incomprehensible, so I'll leave it for now and try to express the view of several thoughtmeisters in this field.

Most people are aware that the brain works by electrical stimulation of neurones, and that different but adjoining neurones have junctions between them over which the tiny current must "fire".

That's the common knowledge part, but the great leap here is to suggest that this electrical firing vibrates nearby molecules in such a way that the thermal bath scenario described above actually occurs in the brain. This, of course, requires the input of energy.

This would explain why, when energy ceases to be pumped into the brain, we "lose" consciousness, which is replaced by unrelated, illogical experiences which bear little relation to the "real" world we physically inhabit. These "dreams", as we call them, are quantum super-positions of possible infinite realities which may possibly be realised in future (or past!) experiences.

So, we currently have a picture of consciousness as a coherent ground state, uniform in space and persistent in time – the "clean slate" upon which all our disparate sensory input is integrated.

So far, this Bose condensed phase seems to rely upon the physical brain for its existence, upon the vibration of molecules in the neurone cell walls emitting virtual photons in a highly coherent fashion. But what happens when the brain ceases to function, as in death?

There is evidence, through personal experience and documentation of such cases, that consciousness can operate independently of the human brain, for example, during N.D.E.s.

I would propose that this is indeed the case. Perhaps once the brain starts to function at birth, and once the highly condensed phase required for the ground state of consciousness is initiated, the latter effectively takes on a life of its own purely from the perspective of our three-dimensional reality. It becomes self-sustaining, not only acting as a receptacle for sensory input throughout physical life, but being solely responsible for the all-important sense of self of which we are all aware, far too complex an experience to be generated by a system of algorithms within the brain alone. This constitutes the ultimate holistic experience.

However, this only accounts for our experience within the three-dimensional physical world.

Many people believe that a person's consciousness possesses a certain duality in a higher and a lower sense, a sort of Jekyll and Hyde, if you will, but in the context of this work, the lower consciousness is the part of our consciousness which interacts with the material reality we happen to be embedded in at the time – the Bose condensate just described – whereas the higher consciousness exists outside time as we perceive it.

These concepts were based on the teachings of the first century schismatic Christian sect known as the Gnostics.

Once the lower self realises the existence of its own higher counterpart, he, or she, breaks free of the physical "prison" they have so far inhabited. They believed reality was an illusion, "Maya", as Eastern religions would have it, and to a certain extent, they were right.

To place the concept of the higher and the lower consciousness on a slightly firmer, if still highly speculative, footing, I will appeal to concepts generated within string theory.

We have already postulated that the ground state of consciousness is formed by the emission of virtual photons by the vibration of molecules in the neurone cell walls. According to string theory, each photon is actually an oscillation on an extended string which inhabits nine spatial dimensions, six of which are curled up in Calabi-Yau spaces. Therefore, consciousness, too, oscillates through these Calabi-Yau dimensions, the part we're familiar with, the lower consciousness, interacting with our three extended dimensions, and the greater part, the higher consciousness, actually inhabiting the six-dimensional higher space.

Is it possible that upon death of the physical brain – the interface with our three dimensions – our cohesive consciousness is liberated for a brief time in the three extended dimensions, giving the experience of rising from the body, and then effectively retreats into the six-dimensional higher space – i.e. the "tunnel" experience – provided by the perceptive cohesion of all the Calabi-Yau spaces? Effectively, viewing physical reality from an "inside out" perspective?

Some N.D.E.ers have remarked how "space is different on the other side". A six-dimensional space would account for this phenomenon.

For the average man on the street, the usual way to break free of physical existence is by death, regarded by the vast majority of people as being rather final!

However, I believe consciousness, in the form of a Bose condensate, self-sustaining in nature, once released from its physical constraint, undergoes a fusion with its higher component in the realms of the six-dimensional higher space.

This is akin to a drastic change in perception as the realisation dawns that the previous physical existence was but one miniscule facet of what actually constitutes the real "you", a mere word in a whole set of encyclopaedias.

This change of perception is viewed by the initially still-human mind in terms the lower consciousness can relate to: travelling through a tunnel, climbing a stairway, going through a door, a gate, or going over a bridge. Conceptually, something relating to the existence just experienced.

But then, according to form, a transition into a blissful state of pure energy seems to be experienced, at least in many cases, and reunion with other entities with whom great affinity is felt.

Mystics have described this as the drop absorbing the ocean, as opposed to the ocean absorbing the drop.

Thus, our transition into a six-dimensional realm is realised, and fusion with the higher consciousness, which has been present all along.

However, some entities only make a partial transition, usually for reasons of their own, either due to unfinished business in the physical realm left behind, through a feeling of attachment to a particular part of it, or a reluctance to make a full transition.

These Bose condensates fail to fuse completely with their higher component within the Calabi-Yau realm, and continue to interact with the physical realm, using the six-dimensional matrix as a means of interacting with the minds of physical beings and as a means of instantaneous transport between places and times in the physical realm.

Having failed to integrate with their higher component, they retain the personality traits - complete with flaws – which they had in the physical.

This could be an explanation for ghosts and poltergeists, although I would conclude that very few Bose condensates condemn themselves to this kind of stasis.

So, for the happy majority who integrate, what opportunities can a six-dimensional existence offer? Can they interact with the physical realm and in what sense?

In the discourse which follows, I intend to build a picture of physical reality using ideas from Special Relativity, and then speculate as to how a liberated consciousness can manipulate such a system using the six-dimensional higher space.

5. DANCING IN HIGHER SPACE

5. Dancing in Higher Space.

To progress further, I must return to the idea of a four-dimensional spacetime continuum introduced in 1908 by the Russian/German geometer Hermann Minkowski, one of Einstein's teachers at the Zurich Polytechnic.

This idea enables the rather abstract and counter-intuitive aspects of Special Relativity to be better understood.

Imagine an event at a certain point in space and at a certain time. Now, information from this event would radiate out in all directions at the speed of light, rather like ripples on a pond when a stone is thrown in.

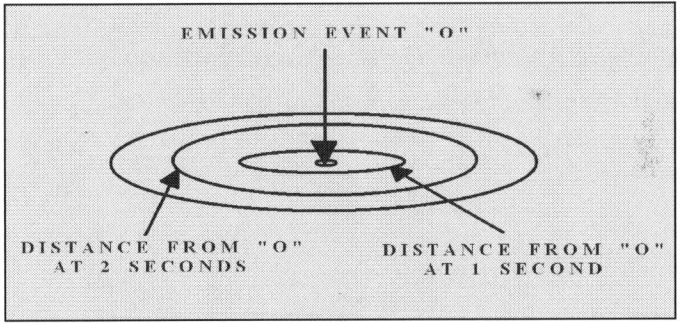

Fig.8. Information Radiates Out At Light Speed From An Initial Event, "O".

To represent this idea in this format would produce a very crowded diagram indeed, so, to clarify this, the whole of space at the time of the event is represented by one snapshot, the whole of space one second after emission by another snapshot, and so on, one laid on top of the other rather like the storeys of a building.

These are termed "simultaneous spaces".

So, the above diagram could be represented thus:

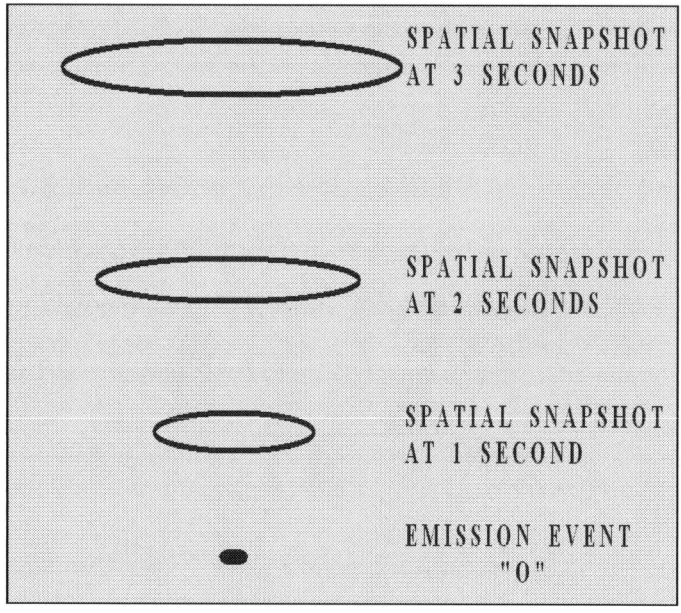

Fig.9. An Emission Event Showing Snapshots in Time.

This is certainly a clearer layout than Fig.8!

Now, to complicate matters just a tad, imagine drawing two lines tangential to each of the radiating circles, starting at the origin.

You would then obtain something like Fig.10 overleaf:

48

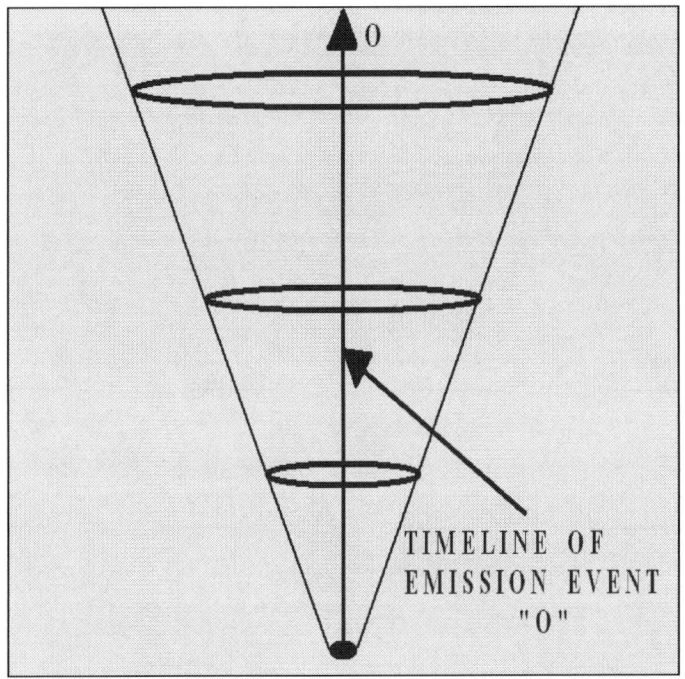

0

TIMELINE OF
EMISSION EVENT
"0"

Fig.10. The Formation of a Light Cone.

This is known as a "light cone". The lines just drawn represent the progression of light radiating outwards from the emission event, and therefore represent the maximum speed attainable: that of light.

A line drawn directly upwards from the original event (which does not move in space, but only through time) represents a stationary object.

Drawn from an "edge on" perspective, we obtain something like Fig.11 overleaf.

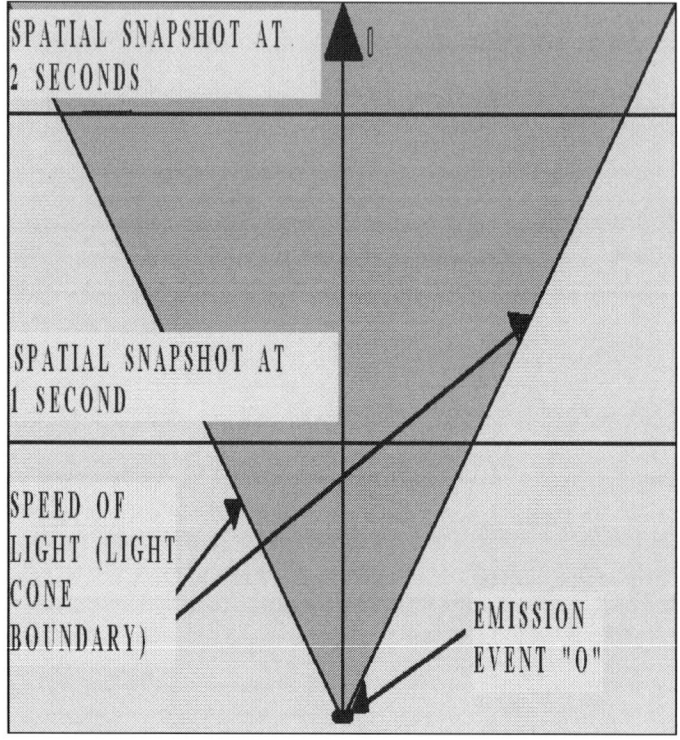

SPATIAL SNAPSHOT AT 2 SECONDS

SPATIAL SNAPSHOT AT 1 SECOND

SPEED OF LIGHT (LIGHT CONE BOUNDARY)

EMISSION EVENT "0"

Fig.11. A Lateral Perspective on Fig.10.

    The central axis can be represented as the progression through time of a stationary object, "O", i.e. its timeline.

    All the area underneath the light cone is outside the zone of information of this particular event, as light/information does not reach this area.

    If you view it from an overhead perspective as in Fig.8, and consider Fig.8 a "snapshot in time", the light will not reach that area until subsequent "snapshots in time". This is what the area underneath the light cone represents.

Now, let's introduce another variable, something travelling at speed, but not that of light. This would be at an angle to the central axis, but within the light cone.

With a singular sleight of creativity usually employed in this type of presentation, let's call it "A"!

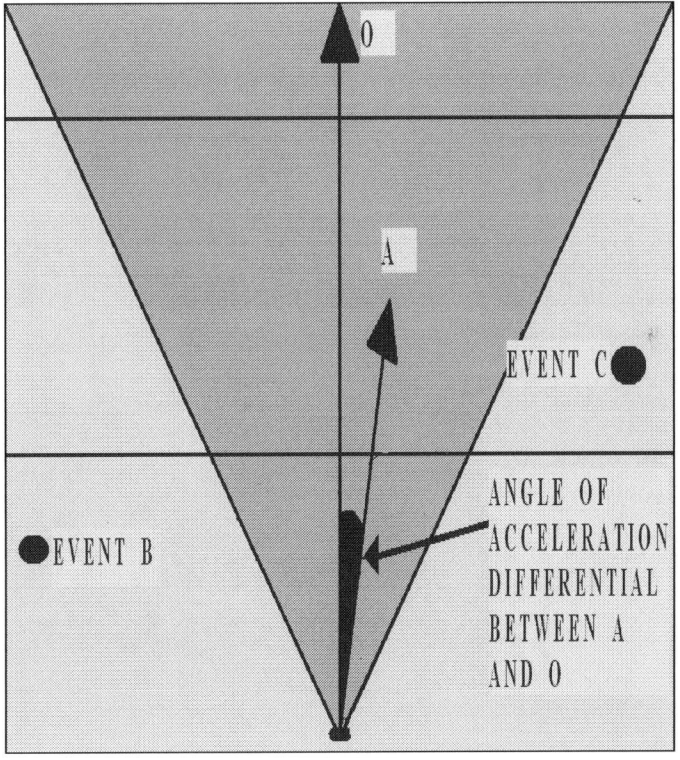

__Fig.12. An Object, "A", Travelling at Speed Relative to "O".__

51

Furthermore, let's introduce two other events, B and C (I'll dispose of the cumbersome speech marks from now onwards!).

Now, to O, as in Fig.12, event B appears to precede event C, but if you take things from A's perspective, the whole frame of reference in which A is involved appears to tilt, from the point of view of O, through an angle related to the speed at which A is travelling, thus we obtain:

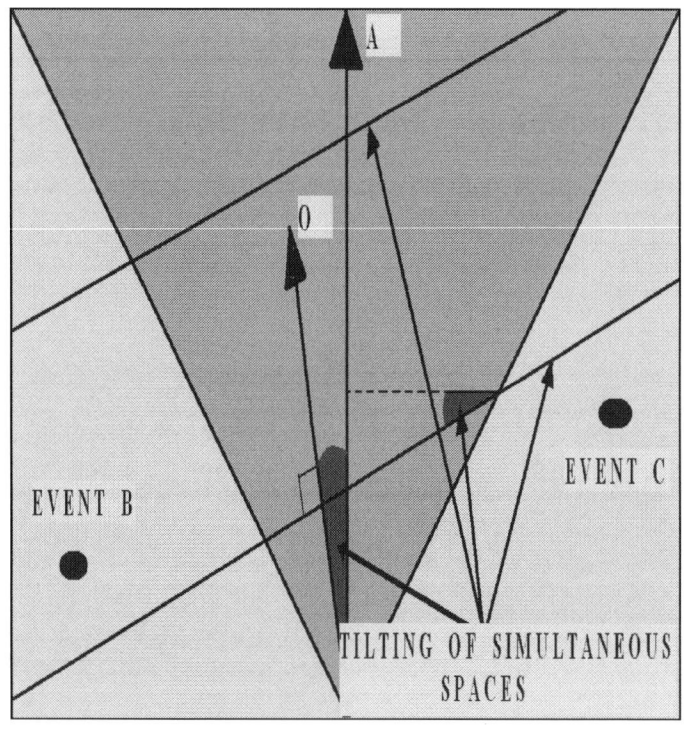

Fig.13. The Tilting of A's Simultaneous Spaces Due to His Velocity.

A is totally unaware of this tilting effect on his simultaneous spaces, but the effects are quite stunning, as you shall see!

As you would expect, the greater the velocity, the more pronounced the tilting of the simultaneous spaces, which is more formally known as a Poincare Motion, after the French mathematician, Henri Poincare.

But look again at Fig.13. According to A, event C now appears to precede event B, as, due to the Poincare Motion on the simultaneous spaces, event C is under the simultaneous space, and event B is above it.

Compare this with Fig.12.

Thus, according to A, a time sequence reversal has occurred from his point of view, even though he's unaware of this!

Remember that B and C don't change their position from Fig.12 – A's perspective has changed.

So, the tilting of the frame of reference represents the distortion of the timing of events according to an observer travelling at speed, and this example illustrates the highly subjective nature of perception of event sequence in the universe.

It may be worth pointing out here that such sequence reversal can only take place with distant events that are outside each other's light cones, so no signal at the speed of light could possibly pass between them. Don't try this at home!

But, if it were possible to send a signal from B to C, hence breaking the speed of light restriction, according to A, this signal would appear to be travelling backwards in time due to the sequence reversal.

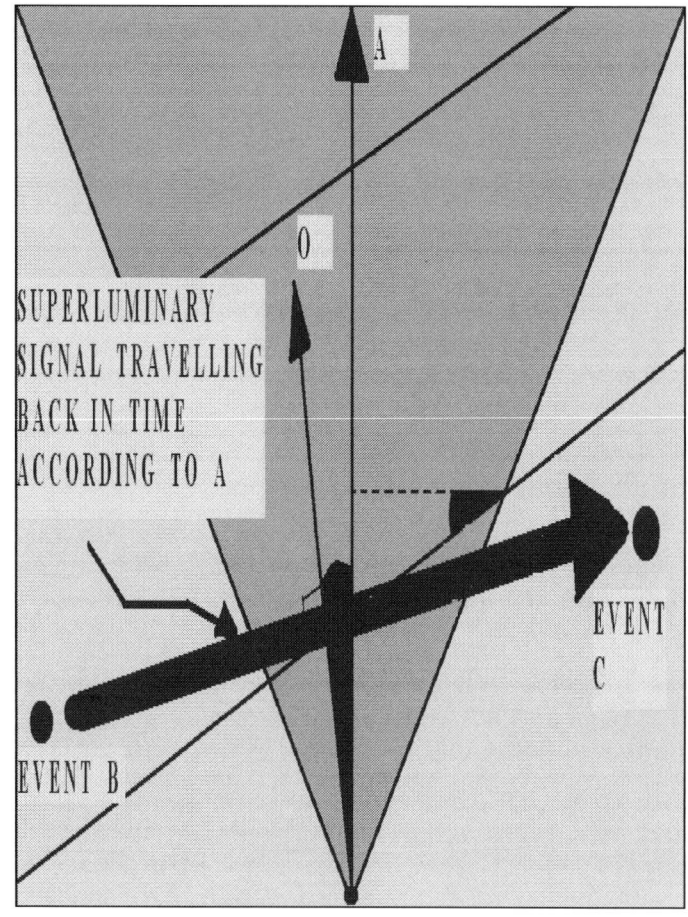

Fig.14. A Superluminary Signal Travelling Backwards in Time.

The point that nothing can exceed the speed of light is fairly well known, but if it is exceeded, some even more anomalous scenarios unfold.

Let's go back to Fig.13 and make some slight(!) adjustments.

Firstly, let us imagine that A is placed quite some distance from O, outside O's light cone, and let's move event B so that it represents an event on O's timeline.

Also, let's make event C an occurrence on the timeline of another object/person outside both O and A's light cones, travelling away from A in the opposite direction from O.

We'll call this traveller D.

So, we obtain something like Fig.15 overleaf, drawn from A's perspective again, remembering that according to A, the signal travelling from B to C appears to be travelling back in time.

Now imagine that D, upon receipt of the super-luminary signal from O at event C, reflects the signal back at the same speed.

To preserve symmetry according to special relativity, the two angles (which correspond to the Poincare transform angle) shown in Fig.16 overleaf must be equal, so this signal is reflected in such a way that this too, according to A, travels backwards in time but in the opposite spatial direction.

Now would be a good time to refer to Figs.15 and 16 overleaf.

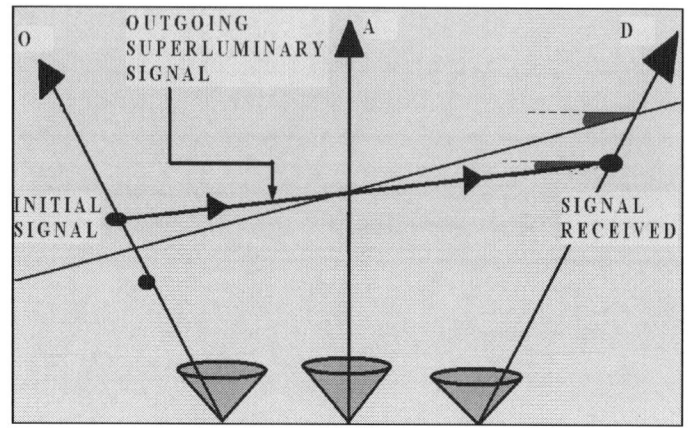

Fig.15. Re-Drawn. Superluminary Signal Travelling Backwards in Time.

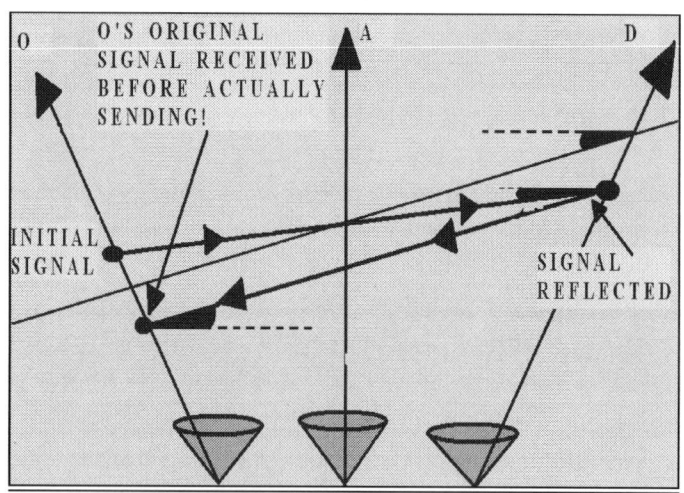

Fig.16. The Reflected Signal is Received on O's Timeline BEFORE He Transmitted It.

Now, look closely at Fig.16. The original signal transmitted by O at event B is, from A's point of view, received by O earlier in time than his original transmission!

In other words, even before he thought of sending his original message, he receives the same message, as the signal has been travelling back in time, according to A, for its outward and return journeys.

Conventional physics uses these examples to show that super-luminary communication would introduce too many anomalies into our picture of the world. But this is the physical world. What about the higher dimensional world of pure energy that the higher component of our consciousness inhabits – the Calabi-Yau complex?

There is a possibility that consciousness is able to transcend the frame of reference in which the speed of light restriction applies, perhaps through the use of the six-dimensional higher space, and in this way, it is able to manipulate the space-time continuum in such a way that it can impinge at any time and any place in the universe instantaneously and simultaneously. After all, we have already speculated that the higher consciousness stands above the time dimension in which its physical component is immersed. Time as we understand it has no meaning for our higher selves.

So, what could be the physical process for this manipulation?

Let's use Fig.16 to build up a picture.

Imagine that O represents the consciousness of a particular person experiencing a particular lifetime in the everyday physical realm – the facet of the Bose-Einstein condensate interfacing with three-dimensional reality – the lower consciousness.

Now, also imagine that A and D represent the part of the Bose condensate which inhabits the higher six-dimensional Calabi-Yau realm, but still connected to this particular person's consciousness – in effect, his/her higher consciousness.

Just as we in the physical three-dimensional realm find it relatively easy to walk from room to room within our houses to get a change of scenery, the Bose condensate in the higher six-dimensional space can easily perform Poincare transforms just described to interact with various time sequences in the physical realm of its lower component.

The A component is able to manipulate the flow of time in the physical realm relative to itself – rather like rewinding or fast-forwarding a tape – to attain the point of interest.

Simultaneous interaction with the D component is then brought into the equation to effect communication with the lower consciousness in the physical realm – the central triangle in Fig.16. Receptivity by the lower consciousness at the earlier point on his timeline could account for phenomena such as precognition, or déjà vu. It is even possible that point C may represent a direct intervention by one's higher consciousness into the mind of its lower counterpart in order to effect a decision which could change the future course of its physical life. Perhaps the imparting of a profound truth or idea (spiritual infusion), or something more mundane like preventing the lower consciousness from making a poor career decision.

Perhaps even interaction on a physical level could take place in this way – manipulation of events producing coincidences or synchronicity.

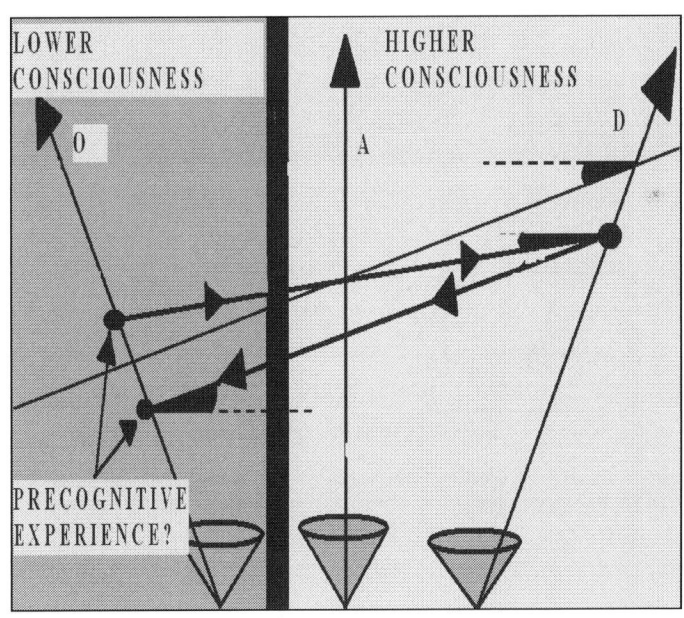

Fig.17. Division into Realms of Higher/Lower Consciousness.

This idea, highly speculative though it is, can certainly open up a whole eternity of potential.

An Eastern mystic and a master of the art of astral projection, Swami Panchadasi, seemed to dwell in this realm when he said:

"By travelling to a point in time, on the fourth dimension, you may begin at that point, and see a moving picture of the history of any part of the earth (universe?) from that time to the present – or you may reverse the sequence by travelling backwards."

On this track, let's take yet another leap of imagination. So far, we have considered this idea in terms of one particular individual experiencing one particular lifetime in conjunction with his component of consciousness in higher space.

But why restrict the higher/lower consciousness partnership to just one life experience? Why not experience and interact with many lifetimes in the physical realm simultaneously (from a higher space point of view)? After all, we have already suggested that existence of our consciousness in higher space takes place outside time as we perceive it in the physical realm – refer to Ouspensky's comments earlier in the text. A similar scenario to that described in Fig.16 could account for reincarnation experiences recounted by various people. For this idea, the O component in Fig.16 would have to be divided into many life sequences and the triangular communication path reversed.

Taken to an extreme, a whole lifetime of experience in the physical realm can be reduced to nothing more than a passing thought in the sophistication of the six-dimensional existence of the higher consciousness.

To expand this idea still further, why would the higher aspect of a person's consciousness exist in isolation? Is it possible that interconnectedness exists between our personal higher self and everyone else's living (and dead in the context of the three-dimensional physical realm)?

If such an interconnectedness does indeed exist, we open up to an idea not just of unity within a particular consciousness, but unity of all consciousness – a super-consciousness, in effect.

Why a unified higher consciousness – a super-consciousness – requires a physical aspect to its existence, I intend to come to – at length! – later. But how is a physical existence experienced when the higher component of our consciousness exists in a higher dimensional realm of pure energy?

For this, I intend to invoke the idea of the energy/momentum 4-vector.

Initially, I will run over the general conventional idea of what exactly an energy/momentum 4-vector is, and then I will expand this initial idea to accommodate the much wider meaning for the concept of the energy/momentum 4-vector which I intend to use for this book.

I hope, by the way, that the reader did not find this short section on relativity too daunting!

After all, most people tend to go weak at the knees at the mere mention of its name, but the reason I have included a section on it is to develop a scenario which the ideas in this book can hopefully transcend and put into perspective as a characteristic of the physical plane only, not the mental one, which goes much, much deeper.

6. HITCHING A RIDE ON A

REALITY

6. Hitching a Ride on a Reality.

In Newtonian physics, the mass of an object quantifies the matter it contains. Moreover, mass is conserved, i.e. the mass, hence the total matter content, of any system whatsoever must always remain the same.

But, according to special relativity's E=mc2, mass and energy are inter-convertible.

When an atom decays, you will find that the mass of the resulting products of decay, when added together, is actually less than the original total mass of the original atom.

However, when the kinetic energy of the resulting products of decay is calculated, and converted into mass by division by c squared, adding the result of this conversion to the actual mass of the products results in obtaining the same figure as the total mass of the original atom.

Thus, mass is not quite the immutable measure of quantity of matter that it was in Newtonian physics, being partly composed of energy.

Furthermore, the energy of a system depends upon the speed with which that system is travelling. If we are at rest watching a particle whizzing along at great speed, its observed energy of motion is considerable. But if we are whizzing along with the particle, its apparent motion – hence its kinetic energy – is zero! This "lost" energy is now viewed as mass by E=mc2.

Thus we are led to the strange scenario whereby the energy (and hence mass, by E=mc2) of a system depends upon our own frame of reference relative to that system.

This is where the energy/momentum 4-vector comes in. This is essentially a Minkowskian geometrical object which measures the inter-conversion of energy (hence mass) of an object and its momentum (hence apparent speed). I say "apparent" here as its speed is relative to the frame of reference of an observer.

Below is a highly simplified representation.

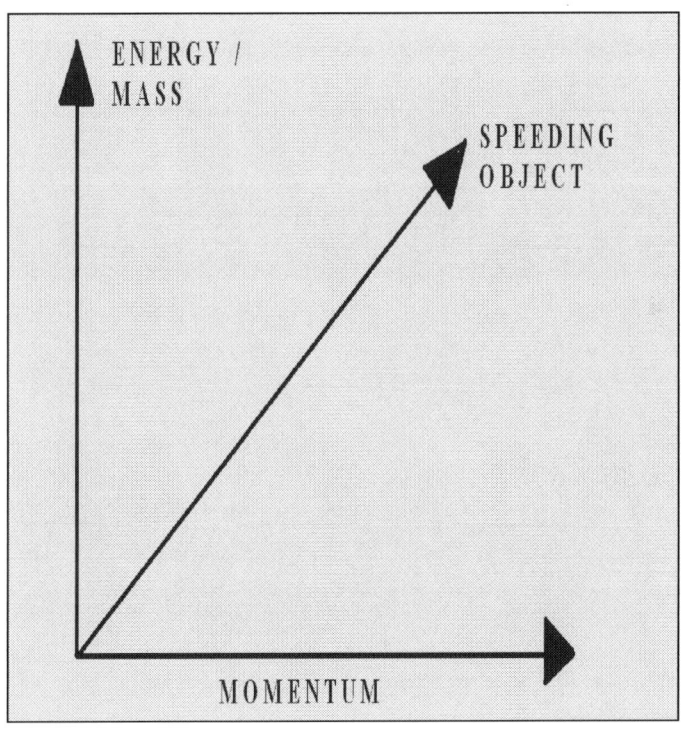

Fig.18. The Energy/Momentum 4-Vector.

Now, the above figure is admittedly a little oversimplified, so for complication, Fig.19 below elaborates somewhat.

Now, Fig.19 gives a very intriguing picture.

If an observer is at rest in space, he follows the time axis at 12 o'clock in the diagram and observes the rapidly moving object as possessing a great deal of momentum. Now, due to the inter-conversion of energy/momentum, the

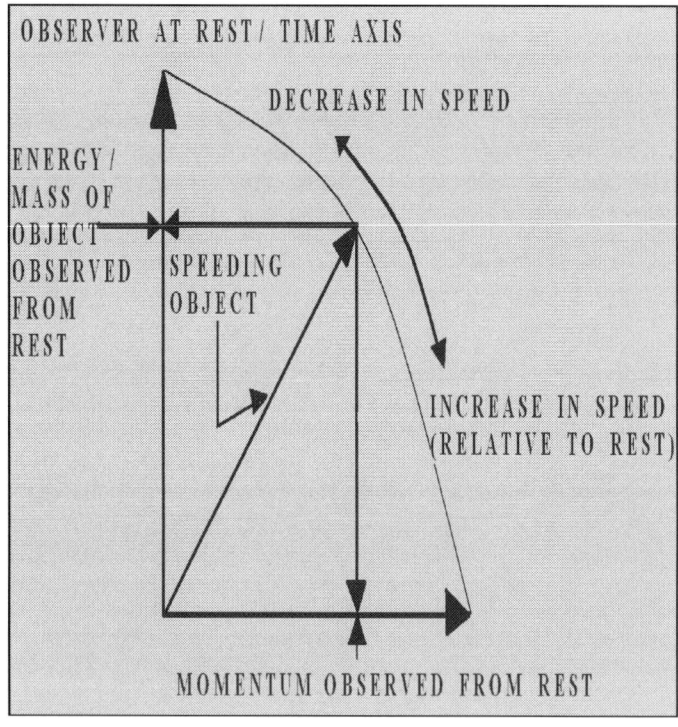

Fig.19. Apparent Mass/Momentum Interconversion.

significant momentum detracts from the amount of observed energy (hence mass) measured on the vertical axis. The faster the object goes, the less energy/mass is apparent – the line to the vertical axis will fall, whereas the line pointing at the horizontal momentum axis will move to the right.

If the object were to slow down, the solid diagonal arrow, representing the object as it actually is, will come closer to the vertical position. As the length of this arrow is fixed (shown by the curve in Fig.19), the line pointing to the momentum axis would move to the left and towards zero (hence no momentum observed), whereas the line pointing towards the vertical energy/mass axis would rise to maximum as the diagonal arrow moved into coincidence with the vertical "observer at rest" arrow. Hence the object would be observed as it actually is when "at rest", with its associated mass/energy.

Now, consider the idea that the diagonal arrow in Fig.19 represents not just one object, but a whole system of objects – in fact, a whole particular reality.

I'll go even further and say that the diagonal arrow represents a particular reality such as the whole physical universe we live in, with all its attendant laws of physics and material objects such as stars, planets and black holes!

Now, for this idea, we need to change the nature somewhat of our energy/momentum 4-vector. The concept used in relativity is actually embedded in four- dimensional space-time. In other words, the red arrow actually represents a particle travelling with a certain velocity through three spatial dimensions relative to another observer, hence balancing apparent momentum with apparent energy/mass.

But if we are to extend the scope of the diagonal arrow to include an entire physical reality with all its attendant laws of nature intact, the diagonal arrow must represent movement on another higher spatial dimension with a quality analogous to momentum from the point of view of our higher consciousness in six dimensional higher space.

By effectively "hitching a ride" (albeit temporarily!) on this diagonal arrow representing a reality, the lower component of consciousness effectively experiences a physical lifetime.

In terms of Fig.19, "hitching a ride" means the arrow representing the point of view of the lower component of consciousness must move into coincidence with the arrow representing a particular reality, hence negating the apparent momentum of the system and maximising the apparent energy/mass of the system.

Now, consider a liberated consciousness adopting a frame of reference at 12 o' clock in Fig.20 overleaf.

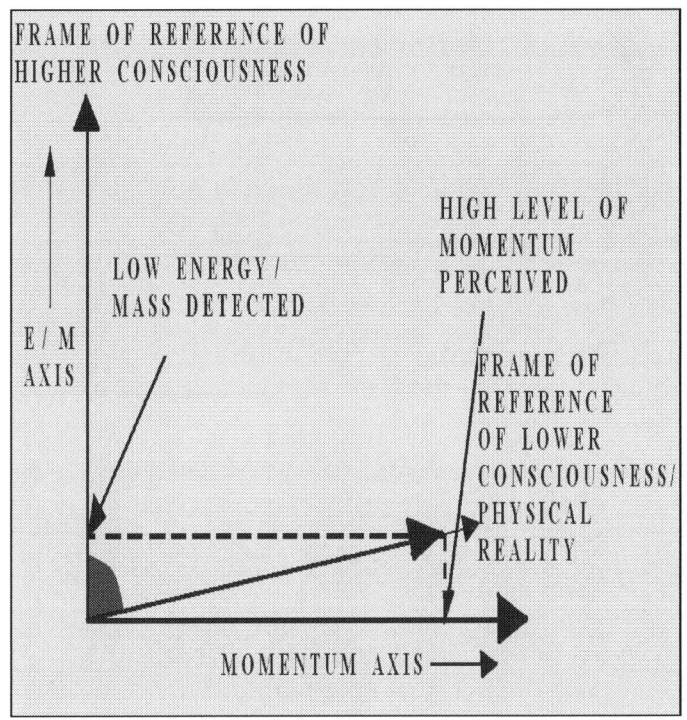

Fig.20. The Higher Self's Perspective on a Reality.

Let's call, for convenience, this particular frame of reference the six dimensional reality of pure energy within the Calabi-Yau spaces.

From this viewpoint, the momentum of the physical reality in question (the diagonal arrow) is seen to be considerable, whereas the detected energy/mass is relatively negligible.

Hence, if the higher self inhabited this viewpoint alone, the reality in question would be barely detectable as a tangible object.

69

But, if the lower component of consciousness were to perform a Poincare transform through the angle shaded in Fig.20, the latter would effectively be at rest (or coincident) with the physical reality concerned which would adopt a totally tangible aspect to the lower component.

To envisage this graphically, turn the black axes of Fig.20 through the shaded angle leaving the diagonal arrow where it is until the vertical axis is coincident with the diagonal arrow as in Fig.21 below.

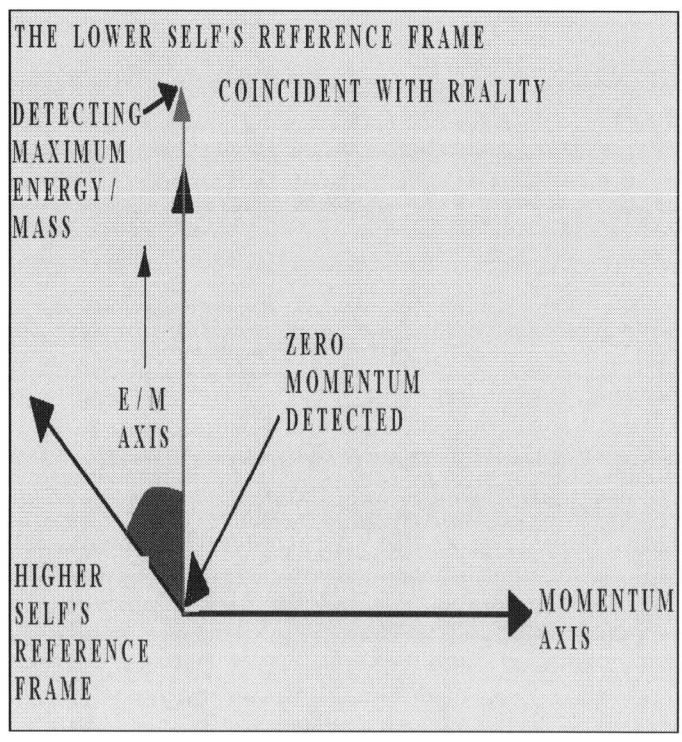

Fig.21. The Lower Self's Perspective.

This should give some insight into my view as to how consciousness interacts with physical reality.

Now, in this situation, the higher component is fully aware of its own existence in higher space, and also of the lower self's existence in the three dimensional physical reality. But in contrast, the lower self, in its temporary immersion in materialistic concerns, is not aware of its higher component until its reintegration upon physical death. The lower consciousness is almost simply a passing thought of its higher component, which expresses the need to experience a physical realm for reasons given later in the text.

So far in the pursuit of this idea, we have only considered one reality. But why limit this? We have already discussed in the introductory section how other realities sometimes seem to impinge on our own. For all we know, there may be an infinite number of realities, all of which can be represented by the energy/momentum 4-vector diagrams already introduced.

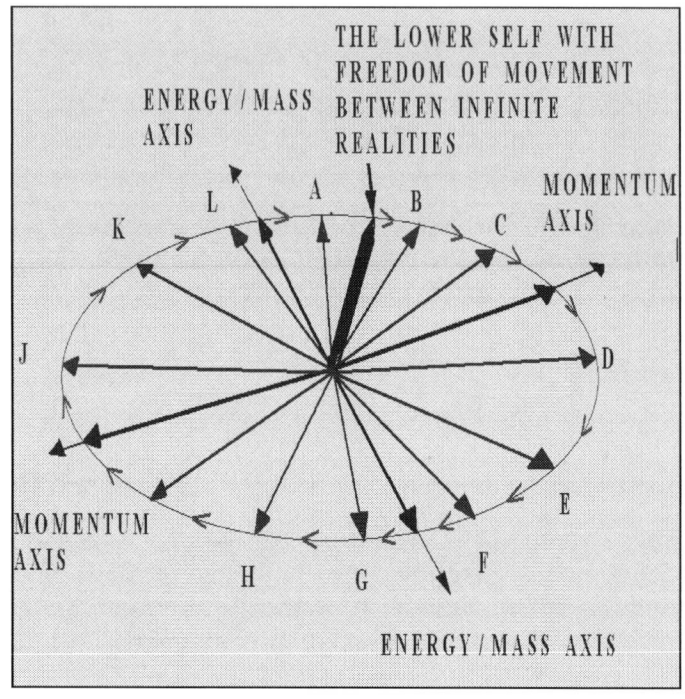

Fig.22. The Star of Infinite Realities.

Have a look at Fig.22 above. Just to represent a few of these possible realities, A, B, C etc., the red arrow represents a liberated consciousness which has freedom of movement through 360 degrees by performing Poincare motions in the six dimensional higher space.

Interaction with a particular reality (only momentarily from the perspective of the higher self) represents the lower aspect of a consciousness, the latter being temporarily unaware not only of its higher form, but also of the other realities in existence.

If infinite realities exist, it is reasonable to suppose that many realities exist which are almost identical except in the most trivial of aspects. Perhaps life decisions taken by the lower self effectively switch its focus between different, but nearly identical, realities all of which exist simultaneously from the viewpoint of the six dimensional higher space. Remember, the higher consciousness exists outside the concept of time as we know it, and above the realm of physical realities.

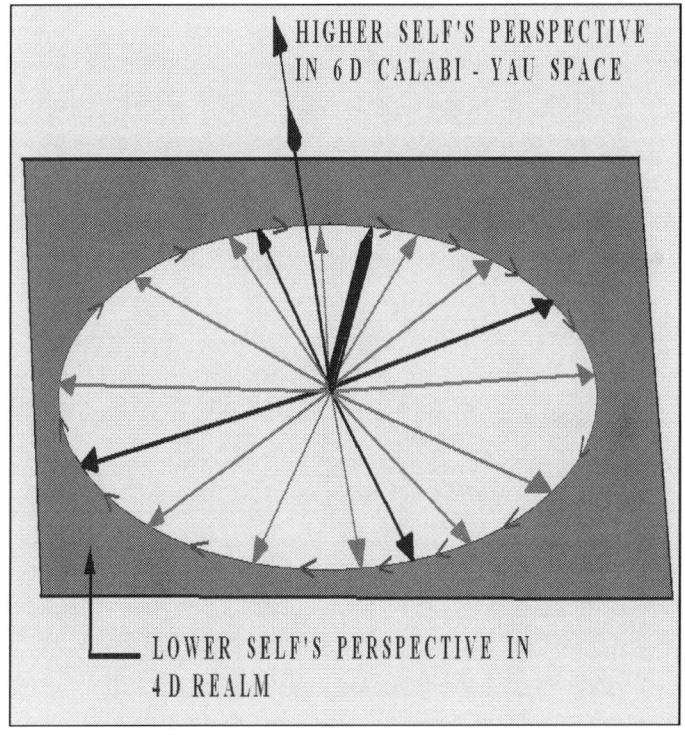

Fig.23. The Higher Self's Perspective.

Now in Fig.23 above, the higher self's perspective is actually drawn as existing above the plane of physical realities which is the actual case.

Now in Figs.20 and 21, the higher self's frame of reference is actually represented as existing on the same plane as the physical realities and the lower self's frame of reference.

This was done purely for the sake of simplicity of illustration, to show how a Poincare motion on the part of the higher self enables its lower component to synchronise with a particular reality.

I hope the reader isn't too misled by this, but Fig.23 represents the scenario I'm attempting to put across and we'll stick with that idea from now on, particularly later in the text in our discussion of Hilbert space, when the idea will be better developed!

I fully believe that we are constantly switching between realities as we go through physical life, but bear in mind that a lifetime for the lower self represents only a particular instant of concentration or "thought" on the part of its higher component.

As all these realities exist simultaneously, it is reasonable to suppose that all possible life paths for the lower self also exist simultaneously.

In one reality, I may be reading this book written by you, whereas in another, neither of us could harbour these ideas. Hopefully, you get the picture! But as beings in the physical realm, we are only aware of one life path at a time.

This concept brings us neatly into the realm of quantum physics, which I intend to invoke to illustrate the great possibility of multiple realities, and a suggestion as to the mechanism to produce them.

But before I move on, I just wish to make an interesting observation regarding the multiple realities diagrammatically represented in Fig.22.

Consider Reality A. If the higher/lower partnership were to perform a Poincare motion and react with this reality, the energy/mass level of this reality would be maximised from the lower self's viewpoint (refer to Figs.20 and 21 earlier).

However, this motion would also effectively raise the energy/mass level from the lower self's viewpoint of the neighbouring reality B, as the angle between the perspectives is reduced.

Could the impingement of other realities on our own be due to a higher apparent energy/mass level of the realities closest in energy levels (or vibrational level!) to that of the one we happen to inhabit?

So! On to quantum physics!

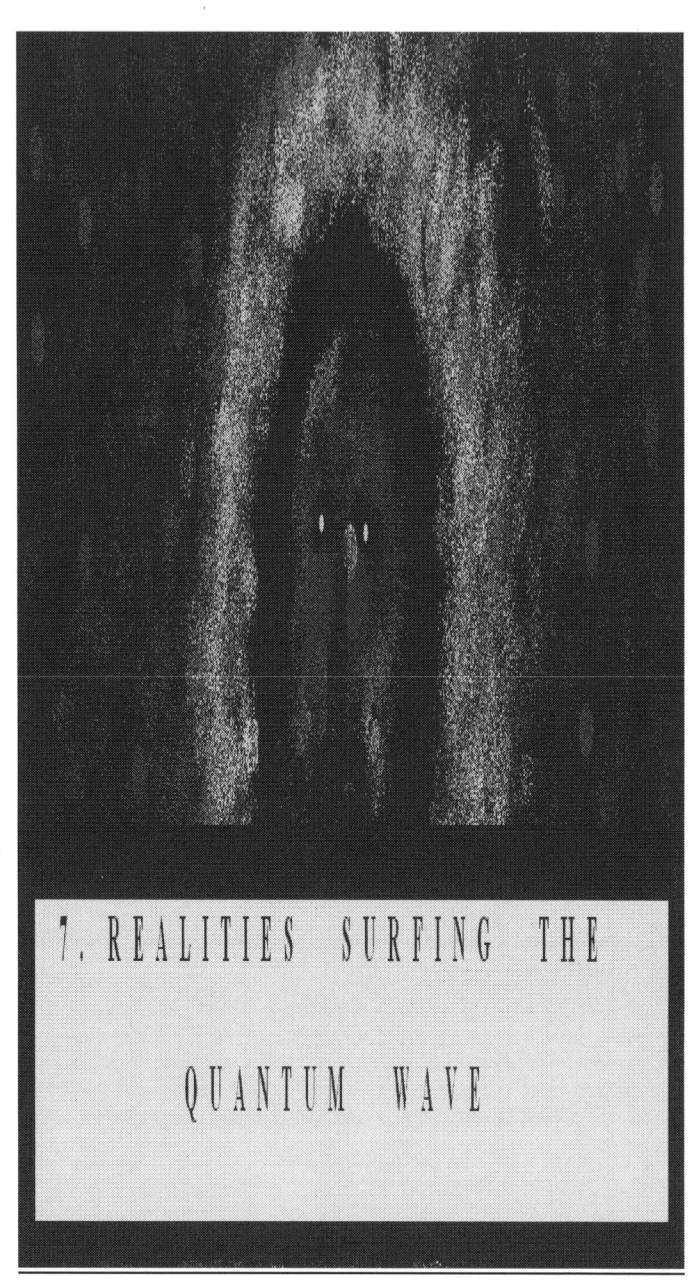

7. REALITIES SURFING THE

QUANTUM WAVE

7. Realities Surfing the Quantum Wave.

To begin our foray into quantum physics, we must introduce the idea of the two slit experiment, devised in the early 1800s by a physicist called Thomas Young.

He used this experiment to establish that light actually consisted of waves, although Isaac Newton had insisted that light may be particles.

In 1900, Max Planck proposed that electromagnetic oscillations occur only in "quanta" (i.e. particles).

Einstein, too, insisted that the electromagnetic field exists in discrete units.

Yet the two slit experiment seems to confirm that light actually behaves as waves.

Let's have a brief look at this experimental set-up.

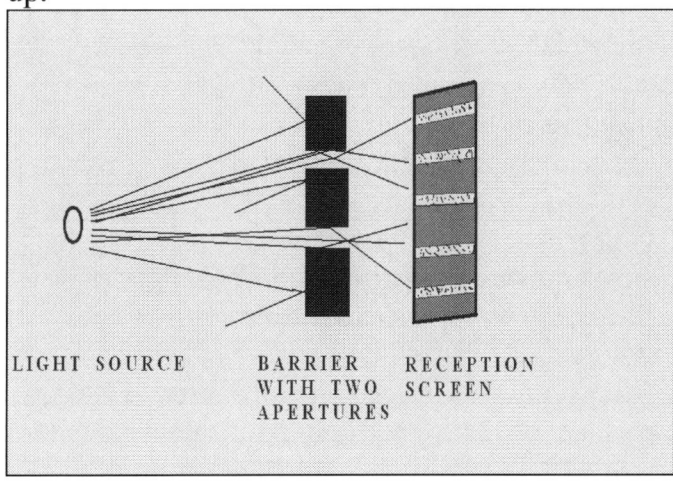

LIGHT SOURCE   BARRIER   RECEPTION
                        WITH TWO   SCREEN
                        APERTURES

A light source is shone at a barrier with two narrow apertures through which light can pass. At the other side of the barrier is a screen which receives the light passing through the two slits. This displays light and dark bands where the wave patterns interfere with each other. Where the waves reinforce each other, when they are "in phase", a light band occurs.

However, where the waves cancel each other out, when they are "out of phase", dark bands occur.

These concepts are known as "constructive" and "destructive" interference respectively.

Of course, there are intermediate phases but we'll ignore these for the sake of clarity!

Taken purely on this level, this is fairly easy to understand – water waves would behave in exactly the same way if passed through two narrow slits.

Thus, it appears that light behaves as a wave. Clear cut, eh?

But hang fire! Newton, Einstein and Planck proposed that light actually consists of particles.

So, let's look at the two slit experiment on these terms.

Let's close one slit, and just have one slit open. On closer observation, light is indeed observed to arrive at the screen in discrete quanta, but it does exhibit wave-like behaviour.

As it passes through the slit, light spreads out by diffraction, a feature of wave propagation.

But a particle picture still holds. The pattern on the screen only appears smooth because of the vast amount of individual photons involved. If the intensity is reduced, the pattern is indeed seen to be formed of tiny dots.

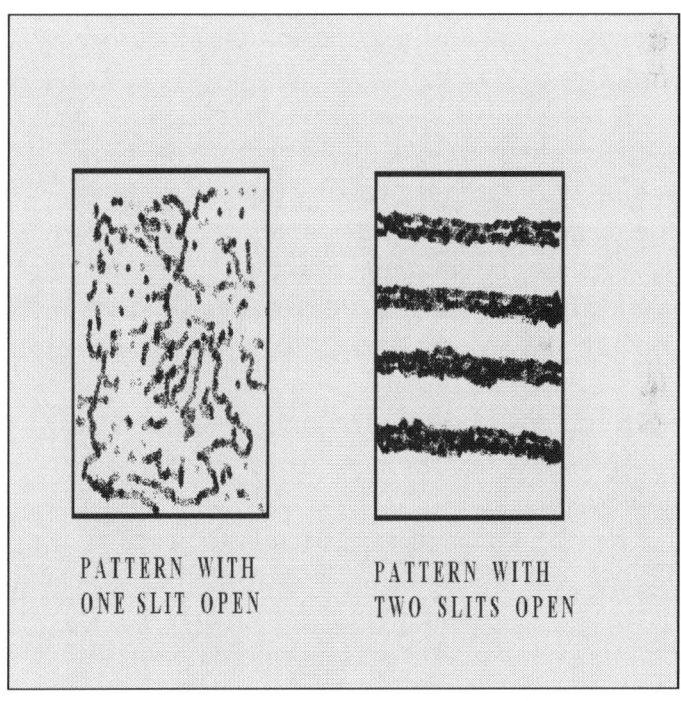

PATTERN WITH
ONE SLIT OPEN

PATTERN WITH
TWO SLITS OPEN

Fig.25. Surprising Results on the Right.

However, when both slits are open, we get a wavy pattern of dark and light bands with bands of zero intensity, which means in these areas, no photons are arriving at all!

If the light were behaving purely as particles, surely some particles would arrive at the bands of zero intensity, but none does!

Therefore, a wavelike behaviour is implied, as opposed to particle behaviour.

Furthermore, if the light intensity is reduced to such an extent that only one photon is released at a time, this same behaviour is exhibited, which implies the rather disconcerting idea that the photon is interfering with itself!

To make this strange idea a bit clearer: if one aperture alone is open to the photon, then the photon will naturally enough travel through it, and if the other aperture alone is open, then it will travel through that one, but if both apertures are open, then it seems that it travels through neither!

Thus, the photon appears to be behaving as a wave all by itself!

However, this description does not merely apply to photons. It can apply to electrons, protons, neutrons or any other form of particle.

The idea that a particle has numbers of alternatives open to it, some of which cancel each other out, and some of which reinforce each other, is known as quantum superposition. In other words, all the possible routes which the particle could take exist in a superposed state, a realm of possibilities.

But how is this described mathematically? Although I do not intend to delve too deeply into mathematical ideas for the purposes of this book, as such depth would serve no real purpose here, a light foray into a mathematical idea may be appropriate here. I solemnly promise there'll be no equations though!

In the realm of quantum mechanics, every single position that a particle may have – or a route that a photon may take – is an alternative available to it. All these alternatives are combined together using complex number weightings to describe the particle's quantum state – its complex function of position – called its wave-function. This is usually denoted by the Greek letter psi.

Now, this is represented by a horizontal plane denoting a particular position – or route – x,y and a vertical plane called the Argand plane denoted by z which represents the amplitude, or probability, for the particle to be at that particular position, x,y, or take that particular route.

For the sake of simplicity here, I'll depict the probabilities as a three-dimensional bar chart initially, as this is much clearer than the usual format. Imagine the Psi – Curve as charting the top of the bar graph.

See Fig.26 overleaf.

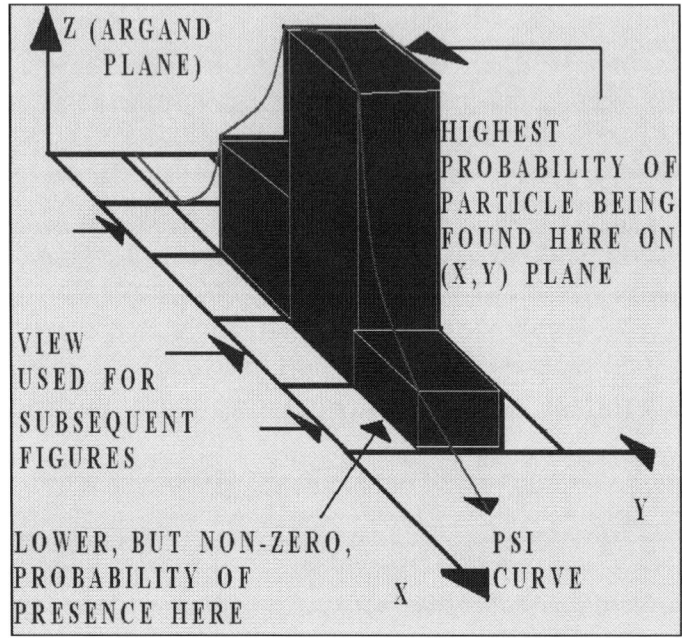

Fig.26. The Psi-Curve in Three Dimensions.

I won't delve into the details of how to work with complex numbers here as this would be counter-productive for our purposes and also I promised not to, but suffice it to say that the "complex number weightings" determine the amplitude of the psi-curve (or the z value) at any point (x,y) on the horizontal plane. We'll leave it at that!

Now, looking at the psi-curve in Fig.26, the points of highest amplitude are the (x,y) positions where the particle is most likely to be found, or, as I said earlier, this can denote the route most likely to be taken, or any other property of the particle. We'll stick with position for now.

However, remember that the psi-curve represents a quantum superposition of possibilities. There is a certain probability that the particle could be found anywhere in the (x,y) plane (representing three dimensional space), but in some places, the probability is higher than in others, denoted by the height of the psi-curve at that point.

But this gives the picture of a particle as being spread out over large regions of space until we happen to take a position measurement, a strange scenario indeed, unless this is viewed from the perspective of multiple realities.

If the reader will now allow me a brief apparent digression into a more detailed description of the psi-curve itself, I will attempt to insert these admittedly complex ideas into some form of nutshell.

The psi-curve just described is actually formed of harmonics, just as a musical sound is. Now, these harmonics actually comprise the different momentum states that the particle could have.

The psi-curve for a momentum state is actually a helix – or corkscrew – wound around the x-axis of Fig.26. The tighter the winding, the larger the momentum described. A momentum state is actually described in the arena of momentum space, so in Fig.26, for instance, the x-axis would be replaced by a momentum axis, p.

Refer to Fig.27 below.

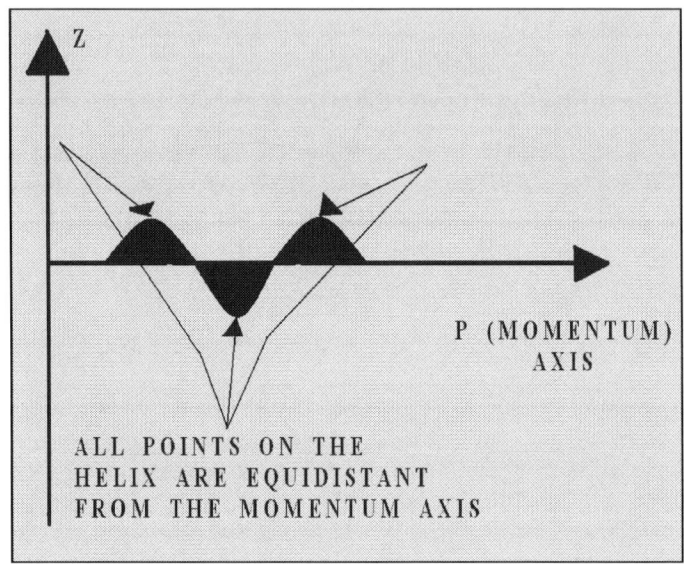

Fig.27.The Psi-Curve in Momentum Space.

Remember that with a "conventional" psi-curve, the distance from the x-axis – the amplitude – represents the probability of the particle being found at that point in the x-y plane, or taking the route represented by that point.

However, looking at the helix above, it is equidistant from the p (momentum) axis at every point along its length, therefore, the momentum represented by the helix is completely indeterminate – nowhere on the p axis is favoured over any other.

Applying what mathematicians refer to as a Fourier transform (again I won't cloud the issue unnecessarily by delving into this!) to the curve in Fig.27, a transposition into a position space arena as in Fig.26 is achieved. But the psi-curve in Fig.26 is formed of a whole panoply of momentum helices (remember the harmonics?) as opposed to the single momentum state depicted in Fig.27, so when the Fourier transform is applied to the latter, a much more defined psi-curve in position space is obtained. This is known as a delta function (a "spike") shown below.

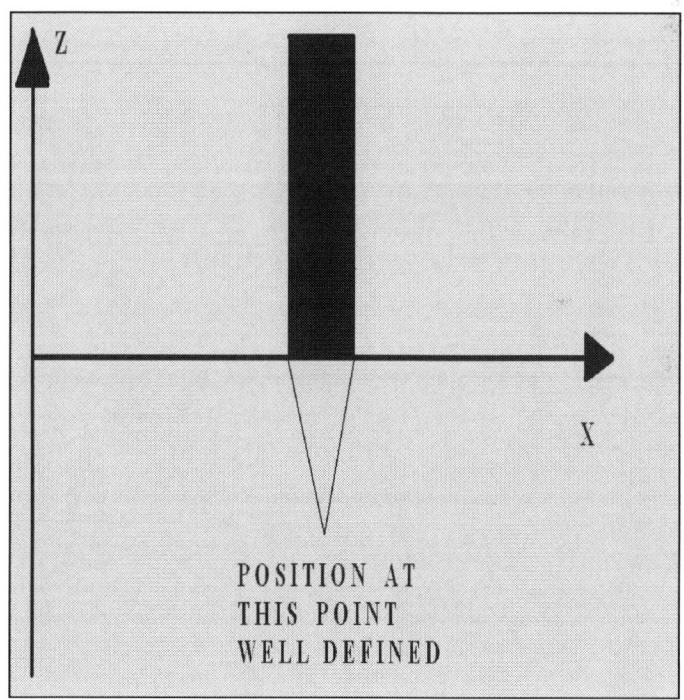

Fig.28. A Fourier Transform Produces a Delta Function in Position Space.

Now, this pinpoints precisely in position space where the particle is. This holds with Heisenberg's Uncertainty Principle, whereby, if a particle's position is pinpointed, its momentum is completely uncertain, whereas if a particle's momentum is ascertained, its position is unfathomable.

In tandem with the last statement, if Fig.28 above depicted the psi-curve as a helix, the particle's location in position space would be uncertain, but a Fourier transform would transpose this to a delta function in momentum space which would pinpoint its momentum exactly, the reverse of the previously described procedure.

Pushing this idea a little further, recall the description of the energy/momentum 4 vector earlier.

The higher consciousness existing in six dimensional higher space, the Calabi-Yau complex, is aware of all momentum states, or potential realities, simultaneously, but not any specific one. Remember that a physical reality is actually a momentum state on a higher spatial dimension that we perceive as time.

Hence, the viewpoint of higher consciousness corresponds to a helix in momentum space with no particular focus on any one physical reality.

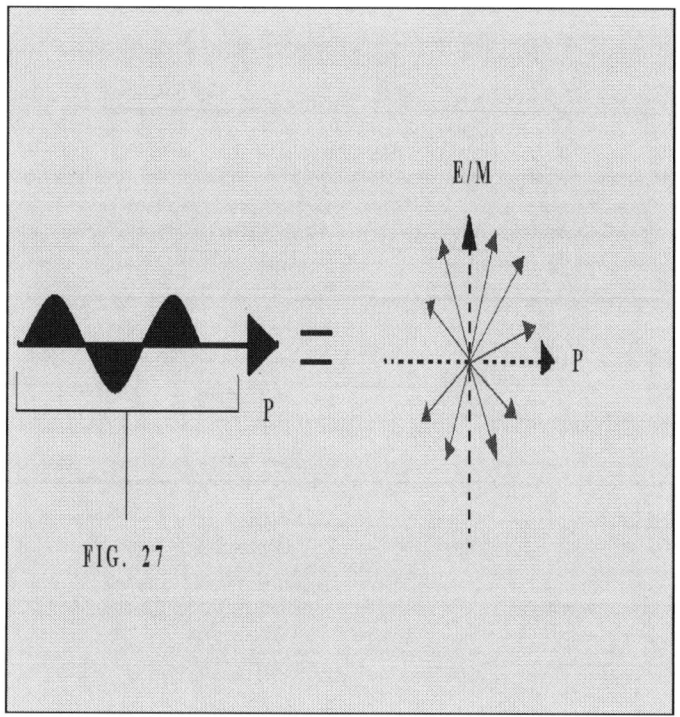

FIG. 27

Fig.29. The Omni-Aware Higher Consciousness.

However, the lower consciousness is "tuned in" to one particular reality.

So, if a Fourier transform is applied to Fig.29 above, a delta function is obtained in position space, as in Fig.30 overleaf.

This transform represents the change of perspective from higher to lower consciousness, and vice versa – a life to death transition.

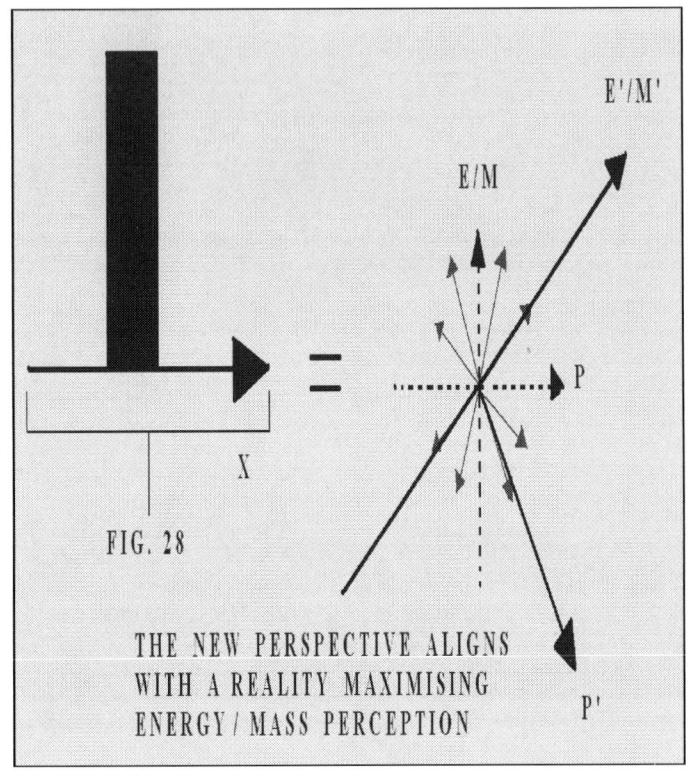

FIG. 28

THE NEW PERSPECTIVE ALIGNS
WITH A REALITY MAXIMISING
ENERGY / MASS PERCEPTION

Fig.30 .The Lower Self's "Tunnel Vision" Perspective.

Returning to the description of the two slit experiment set to just emit one photon at a time, if the photon goes through slit A, its delta function in position space is peaked at that point, whereas if it goes through slit B, its delta function is peaked at *that* point in position space.

But, recall that a photon appears, bafflingly, to be able to interfere with itself, hence, it seems that it is able to pass through both slits at once! In this case, it has a double peaked delta function in position space, as depicted in Fig.31 below.

Moreover, no matter how far apart the slits are, this phenomenon can occur, even when the slits are light years apart!

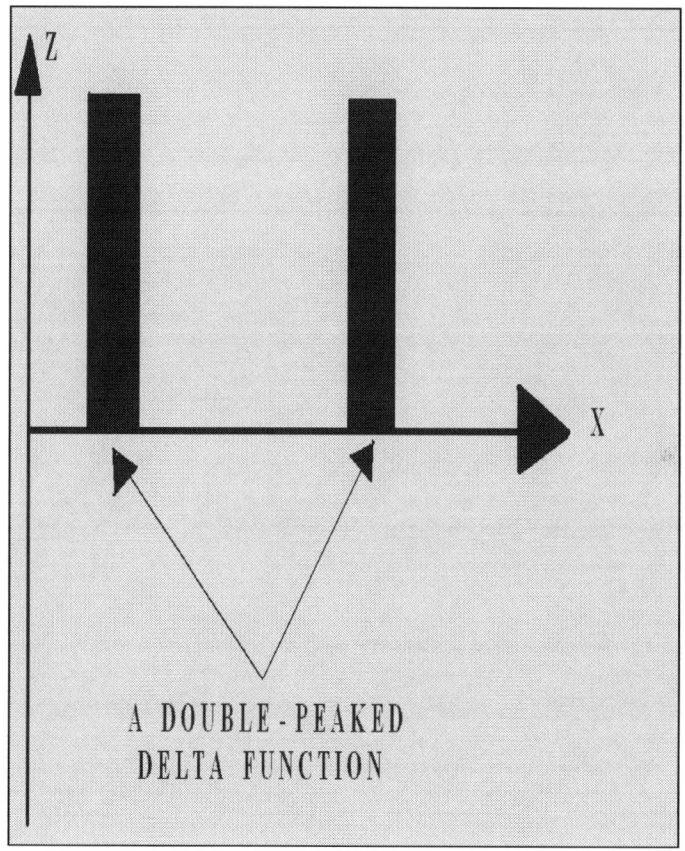

Fig.31. Constructive Interference.

If the wave-functions are in phase, constructive interference occurs as in Fig.31. When out of phase, destructive interference (cancellation) occurs as in Fig. 32.

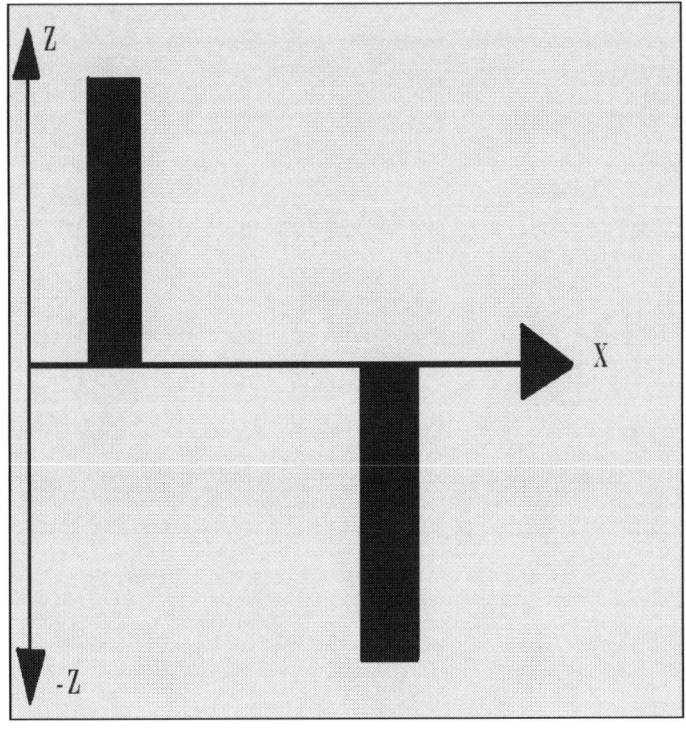

Fig.32. Destructive Interference (Cancellation).

Intermediate phasings can obviously occur, as illustrated in Fig.33 overleaf.

But how can this be? How can one particle interfere with itself?

Only if this same particle exists in separate realities (or sub-realities) which combine in a

***plethora of combinations to construct the reality
we detect around us!***

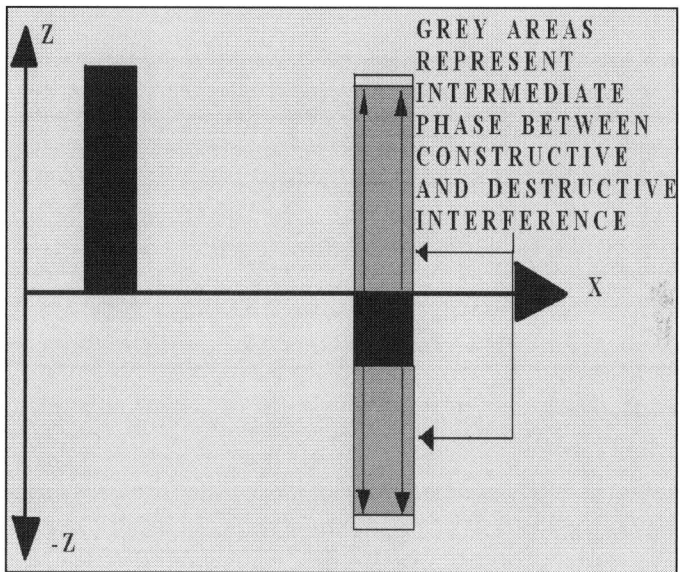

Fig.33. An Intermediate Phasing.

But remember, in the case of physical reality with
which we are all so "familiar", we're not just
dealing with one particle, but a whole universe of
them, all behaving in the manner just described,
forming the macroscopic objects around us, in
the three dimensional space in which we live.

This gives the potential for infinite
combinations of actual realities which, in fact, are
projections into three dimensional space from the
six dimensional Calabi-Yau energy field which
our higher consciousness already inhabits.

These projections take on the form of momentum states containing all the information of the various realities throughout their own timelines, which only become tangible as physical realities when the lower facet of consciousness "hitches a ride" on a certain reality, or momentum state, by the auspices of a (not necessarily) human brain.

This rather flippant idea of "hitching a ride" on a reality has its philosophical equivalent known as "collapsing the quantum wavefunction", or, couched in more precise terms which physicists would prefer, undergoing "state vector collapse".

Recall that all possible realities – all potential scenarios – exist in a state of quantum superposition. In other words, all potential realities exist at once, but we tend, in the physical realm, to unconsciously choose but one.

On a quantum level, all routes exist for the photon and it indeed appears to take all of them, but if we place a detection device at one slit or the other, the photon will be detected at only one or the other.

By taking a measurement, we have effectively collapsed the wavefunction, or the state vector, to choose but one reality over all others.

This is what we do continuously throughout our physical lives, mostly unconsciously, by every decision we take, however trivial, or by the way in which we are affected by other people's decisions.

At this juncture, I would like to introduce the concept of Hilbert space, a mathematical space of infinite dimensions introduced by the German mathematician, David Hilbert, although for our purposes we only need to use ten!

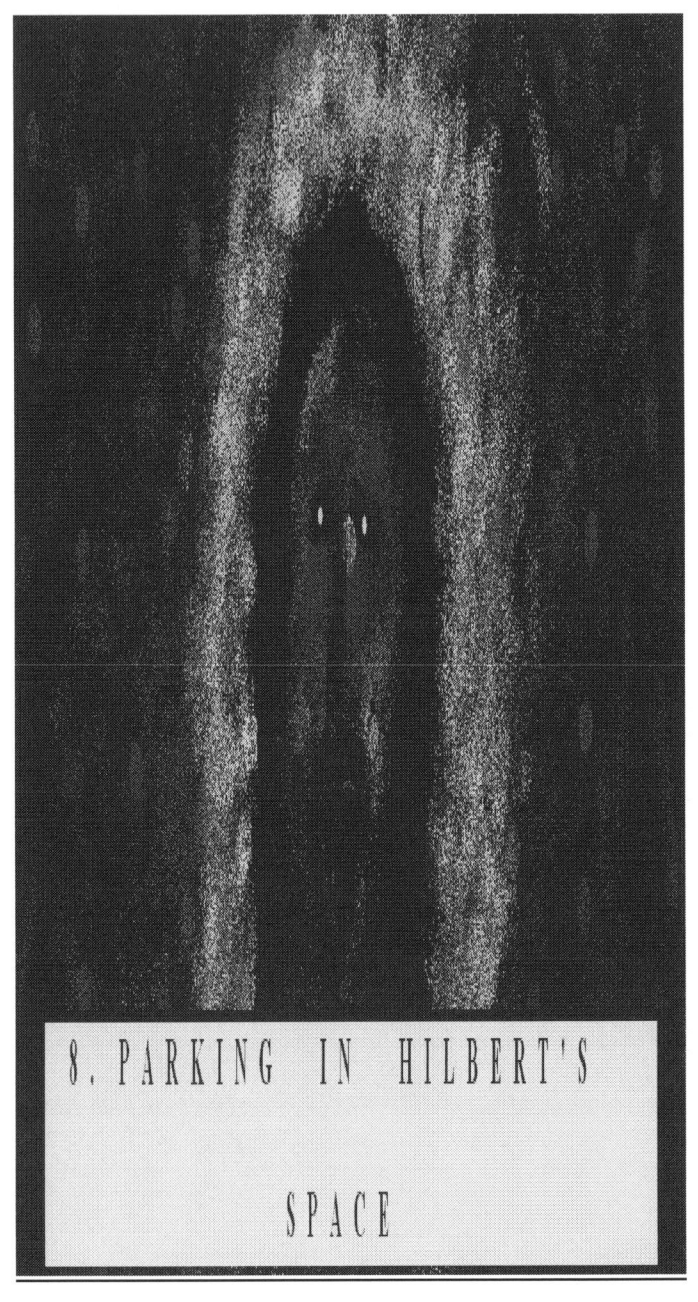

8. PARKING IN HILBERT'S

SPACE

8. Parking in Hilbert's Space.

A single point in Hilbert space represents the quantum state of an entire system. A dimension in this space is not a spatial dimension with which we are familiar. A dimension in Hilbert space represents a certain quantum state of a system which evolves unaffected by other quantum states in other systems.

Hopefully, I haven't lost you already (!), but just in case the mists of incomprehension are descending, a rough analogy would be to say that each dimension of Hilbert space is a thick-walled channel in which quantum events can happen unaffected by quantum events in other thick-walled channels!

This independence of evolution of quantum events is known as orthogonality.

Now, each quantum state in Hilbert space is known as a state vector – let's call this state vector "psi" for convenience.

This state vector represents the system – or reality, for instance – as it really is. For our purposes, the state vector evolves in six dimensional space, and represents the energy field which also contains higher consciousness.

The alternative physical states of this system which constitute the various projections into three dimensional space, our physical realities, are represented in Hilbert space as independent projections on orthogonal basis vectors as shown overleaf.

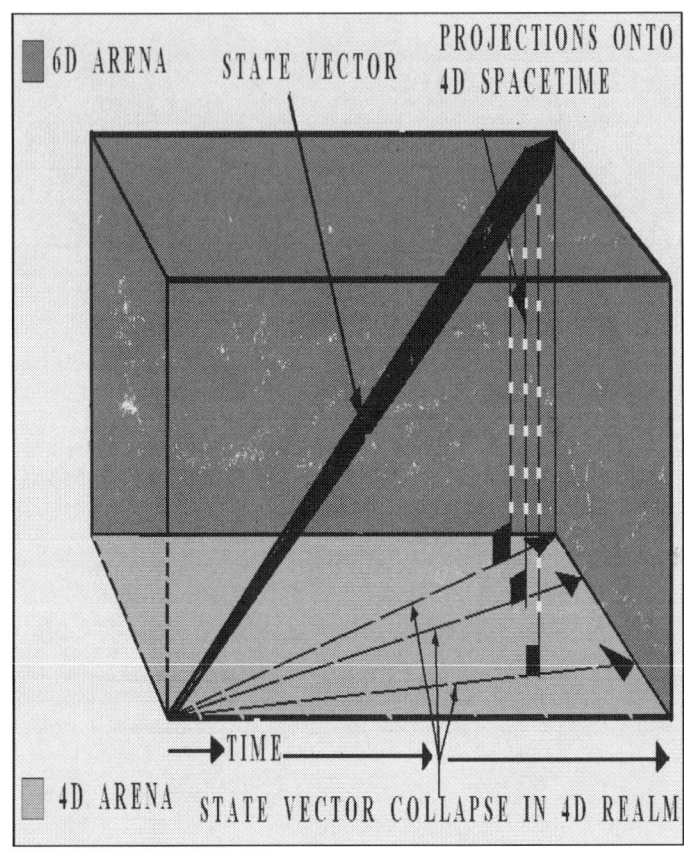

Within the figure:

6D ARENA   STATE VECTOR   PROJECTIONS ONTO 4D SPACETIME

→TIME→

4D ARENA   STATE VECTOR COLLAPSE IN 4D REALM

***Fig.34. Projections from the 6-Dimensional
Energy Field onto 4-Dimensional Space-time.***

For the purposes of clarity, only three
projections, or realities, are shown here, but
remember that there are possibly an infinite
number of these, which would make the above
diagram somewhat crowded!

You may be able to see here a resemblance to
the earlier diagram, Fig.23, repeated below:

96

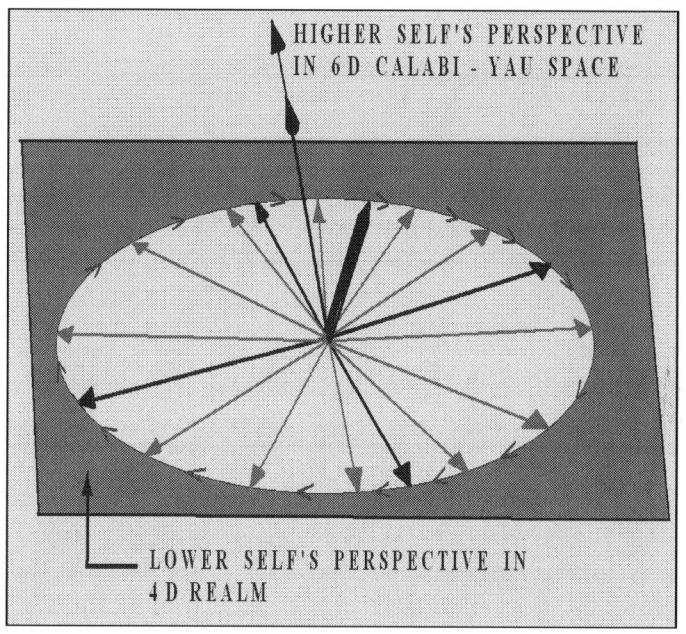

HIGHER SELF'S PERSPECTIVE
IN 6D CALABI - YAU SPACE

LOWER SELF'S PERSPECTIVE IN
4D REALM

In the "fish tank" of Fig.34, the base of the tank represents the familiar four dimensional spacetime we inhabit in the physical, whereas the full volume of the tank represents the six dimensional Calabi-Yau realm of the bosonic energy field which includes higher consciousness.

The state vector, psi, then, as you can see by comparison with the repeated Fig.23, coincides with the standpoint of the higher consciousness.

A Hilbert space scenario, then, can, very schematically, represent a suggested way in which aspects of the energy field of six dimensional space can be projected into the four

97

dimensional scenario as one of many infinite alternative realities.

Note that in Fig.34, a transition up and down the faint perpendicular lines between the state vector and its projections represents the transition between life and afterlife, or lower and higher consciousness, in the context of this book.

Perhaps here it would be prudent to incorporate some form of summary of what we have so far! So, here goes!

Consciousness interacts with all these realities in such a temporally unrelated fashion that it's difficult to discern this interaction, and reality effectively appears objective, and strictly external to the realm of consciousness.

I believe it achieves this outside the context of physical existence through the medium of the six dimensional higher space represented by the seemingly fragmented Calabi-Yau spaces, which, in fact, form a consistent six dimensional matrix through which all possible physical realities are projected.

High dimensional Hilbert space represents this entire arena as depicted in Fig. 34.

The three dimensional realities all exist interwoven with the six dimensional world. They are not separate entities, but an integral part of the whole scheme, with infinite combinations of energy to matter transforms by means of the energy /momentum 4 vectors described earlier.

The latter describe movement upon a higher dimension, which I propose is that we know as "time", which has a spatial character elaborated upon later in the text.

Life decisions determine which reality we interact with throughout physical existence, even though we're not aware of this constant switching between realities while we're alive.

Perhaps this is why, in past life regressions, certain details appear to be "inaccurate". They are only inaccurate in the context of the particular physical reality experienced by all parties concerned at the point of regression.

I have one final point to make in this section before we proceed to the next section, and that is concerning the Einstein-Podolsky-Rosen paradox, or the E.P.R. paradox for short.

Most of the particles found in nature actually possess a property called "spin". Now, this isn't spin in the ordinary macroscopic sense of the word, such as that applied to a spinning top or a compact disc, but a very discrete quantum state of a particle. For any particular type of particle, the amount of this spin is always the same, but the axis of spin can vary according to which particle is observed.

Electrons, protons and neutrons – the matter particles – have spin ½. These are collectively known as fermions. The remaining particles are collectively known as bosons , and have the property of spin – 1. The latter are all the particles associated with energy fields, such as photons (electromagnetic force), gravitons (gravitational force), gluons (strong nuclear force) and weak gauge bosons (radioactive decay).

Now this concept of spin produces some very strange results indeed!

When a particle decays, the spin of the two component parts must add up to the total spin of the original particle in order for angular momentum to be conserved.

Now, say you confine one of the particles for measurement of its spin.

The axis you choose from which to measure its spin is totally arbitrary – you have free choice.

Yet, amazingly, as soon as you take this measurement of spin, the associated but escaped particle exhibits spin in exactly the opposite direction, on the same axis, whether it is only a matter of feet away or light years away!

This is so angular momentum can be conserved.

This fact can be proved algebraically, but again considering people's general aversion to mathematics, we'll leave that to the experts! The actual algebraic proof can be found in other, more mathematical books than this one!

Now, Einstein objected to this strongly, as the instantaneous fixing of the axis of spin of a particle light years away simply by choosing an orientation of measurement of its partner particle obviously violated the speed of light restriction.

But surely there's a resolution here? Remember all the infinite realities exist in a state of quantum superposition. The choice of measurement on one particle instigates a state vector collapse into a particular reality wherein angular momentum of particles which were once associated must be conserved, however far removed they now are. Also remember that the infinite number of realities will allow for any orientation you wish to choose in which to measure the particle's spin, and the angular momentum will still be conserved.

By choosing your orientation, you are effectively choosing the particular reality projection your life path switches to at that particular moment (remember we switch constantly), with all its history and laws of physics fully integrated and self-consistent, from the formation of the Earth, the extinction of the dinosaurs and right down to the niggly details such as the conservation of angular momentum of the particles in which ever eccentric orientation you choose to measure it from!

In this way, the speed of light restriction remains unbroken, and the laws of special relativity are safe.

Another choice of orientation of spin measurement would simply entail state vector collapse into another reality with all *its* laws of physics and pertinent history fully integrated and self-consistent.

Summary So Far!

What we have so far is a ten dimensional infrastructure, nine dimensions of which consist of space, and one of time, which is itself spatial in nature but not in the usual sense. (This will be entered into shortly.)

Six of the spatial dimensions are undetectable from our three dimensional perspective, and contain a bosonic energy field, partly consisting of a field of consciousness. Infinite combinations of this energy field are projected into the remaining three spatial dimensions and develop, or flow, along the time dimension with a quality analogous to momentum – each reality has a different momentum, which could almost be described as a frequency.

The field of consciousness consists of two components, the higher component, which remains embedded in the energy field in six dimensional space, and a lower component, which can move in tandem with the realities on the time dimension experiencing multiple projections of the energy field into three dimensional space.

When "in phase" with a particular projection, a transform from pure momentum to energy/matter occurs and this is described as a "lifetime". A particular facet of the lower consciousness is only aware of one lifetime at a time, although its higher component is simultaneously aware of them all, being detached from the time dimension as it is.

A very schematic representation is shown below, which is an extension of Fig.34, but incorporating, for clarity, the concept of simultaneous spaces introduced in the section on Minkowskian geometry.

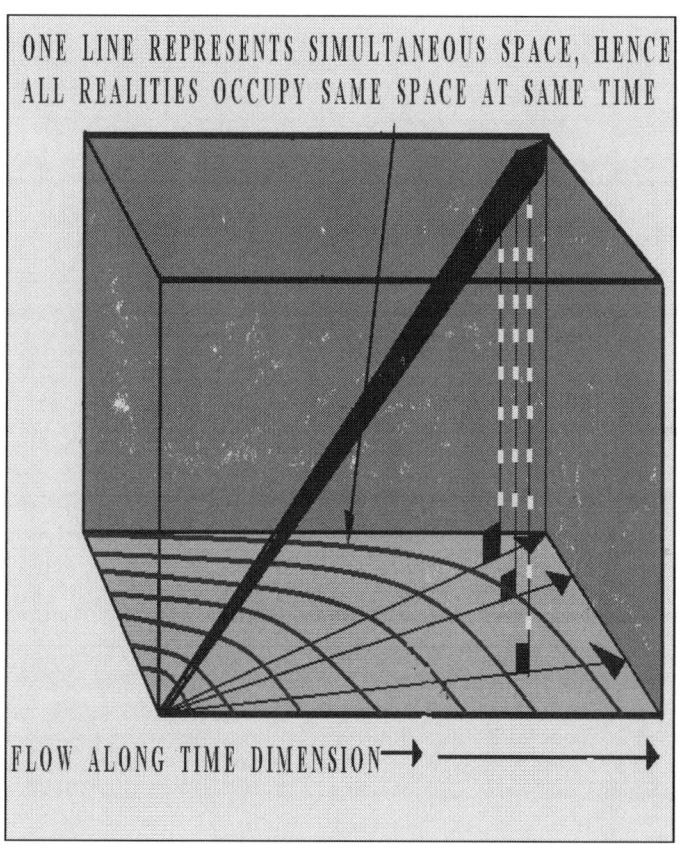

Fig.35. The Ten Dimensional Infrastructure.

Notice that in Fig.32, all the infinite realities occur in the same three dimensional space arena simultaneously, as shown by the incorporation of the concentric lines which represent the simultaneous spaces. Remember that in Fig.9 earlier in the text, the snapshots of the universe at each point in time were represented by ellipses piled on top of each other like the storeys of a building.

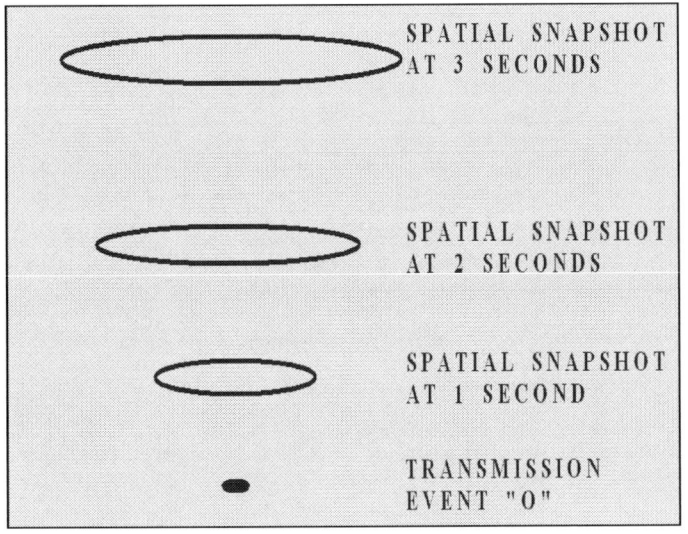

Well, in Fig.35, the time dimension is represented by the base of the "tank" and each concentric line represents one spatial snapshot as shown above, otherwise, the concept is the same.

Also, it would be worth noting at this point that all reality projections and the six dimensional energy field itself, represented as the state vector, all originate at the same point, which in Fig.35 is the bottom corner of the "tank". We'll call this the "origin", O, and we'll elaborate on this further shortly.

So, here's Fig.36, which is Fig.35 with the origin incorporated for clarity.

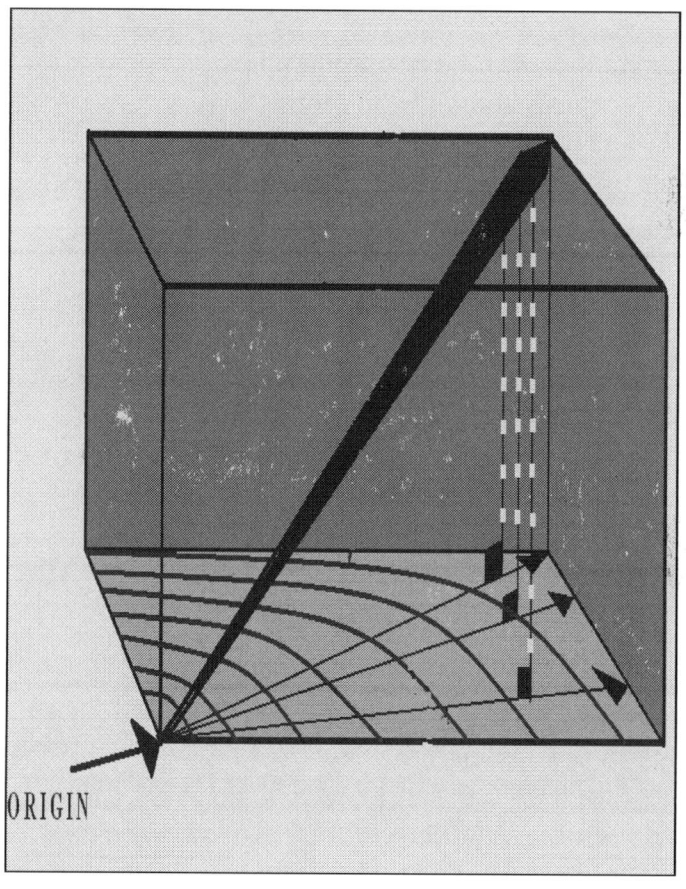

ORIGIN

Fig.36. The Ten Dimensional Infrastructure Showing Origin "O".

In one particular lifetime, our lower consciousness is in phase with one life path only, but this path can transcend different realities throughout life according to decisions we, or others, make.

I have already mentioned that "combinations of the (six dimensional) bosonic energy field are projected onto the remaining three spatial dimensions and *develop* along the time dimension."

How do we mean, "develop"? Well, in effect, *move* along the time dimension as if it were a special case of a spatial dimension, much in the same way that spilt coffee flows across a table top.

But what exactly is movement along the time dimension?

We have already speculated that a reality projection has a quality akin to momentum which is transformed to energy/matter when a consciousness moves with the same "momentum".

But the reality itself also develops, or "grows older", for want of a better phrase, within this scenario, so if you'll allow me a really cumbersome analogy:

Spilt coffee flows across a table surface, but the table is travelling at such a great speed (for reasons unknown!) that you have to match the table's speed first before you can observe the flowing coffee.

So effectively, we have a movement within a movement, a compounded vector! We must eliminate the momentum factor first (match the table's speed) before we can observe the second movement (the flow of the coffee) in the forum of energy/matter.

It is almost as if you need to eliminate the "momentum" factor first before you can peer with increased resolution into the greater detail that the time dimension has to offer, which will be entered into in the next section. This also leads to a striking personal conclusion about the origin, "O" in Fig.36.

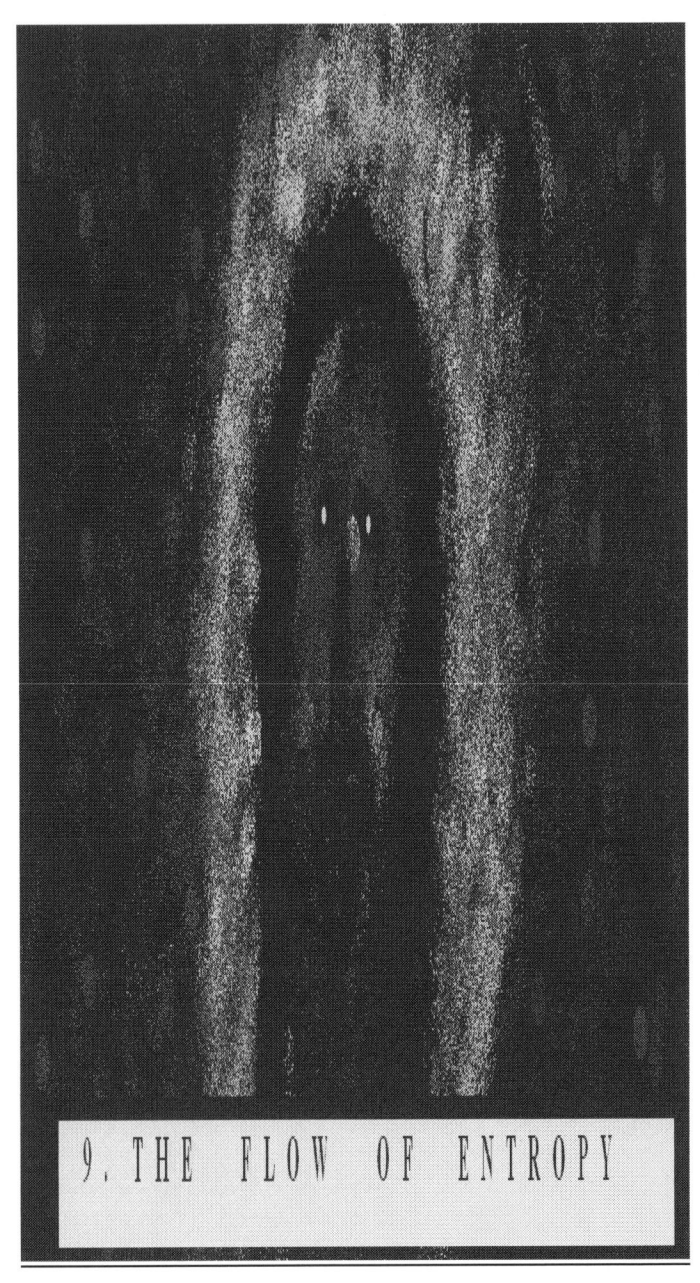

9. THE FLOW OF ENTROPY

9. The Flow of Entropy.

For the next leg of our admittedly involved journey, I need to introduce three major concepts:

The Riemann - Christoffel Tensor,
The Second Law of Thermodynamics and
Phase Space.

Firstly, the Riemann - Christoffel Tensor. This is a mathematical object which describes the curvature of four dimensional space-time, the four dimensions being the familiar three dimensions in which we live, and the dimension of time.

This mathematical expression can be split into two parts: the Conformal tensor, and the Ricci tensor.

The Conformal tensor, very briefly, measures gravitational tidal effects in empty space, whereas the Ricci tensor measures the degree of distortion of spacetime in the presence of mass.

It is the Conformal tensor which will particularly concern us here.

Secondly, the Second Law of Thermodynamics. This states that the entropy of an isolated system increases with time.

So, what is entropy?

Very roughly speaking, it is the disorder manifest in a physical system. For instance, using a relatively simple example, before you boil a kettle, the initial state of the cold water in the kettle is more ordered, or organised. This is said to possess lower entropy.

However, when the kettle is boiled, the steam which issues forth erratically from the spout is in a much more disordered state, much less tightly organised. This is said to possess higher entropy.

Moreover, this process is irreversible in the physical realm we inhabit. The process moves only one way – towards higher entropy.

The universe is moving towards a state of higher entropy all the time, striving to achieve a state of thermal equilibrium where, basically, nothing happens – everything is balanced. You can almost picture it as a tightly wound spring gradually releasing its energy until it is completely relaxed. This completely wound down state is thermal equilibrium, and entropy is the expression of the winding down process.

High Entropy = Thermal Equilibrium/Balance.

This metaphorical spring winding down by the drive towards higher entropy and thermal equilibrium is the engine which drives every process in the physical universes.

Planets move around stars in imperceptibly decaying orbits, ideally to be drawn in to their mother star to be burned in nuclear fusion reactions giving off heat and electromagnetic radiation to be spread in a higher state of disorder, or higher entropy, in an attempt to warm up slightly a cold universe.

Even weather systems on our own planet attempt to achieve this state of equilibrium, air flowing into areas of low pressure in an attempt to even pressure systems out. You no doubt get the picture!

But despite the physical definition of entropy, in what other way could we define this concept? How do we perceive time itself when in the physical realm?

Well, a very broad, crude and personal definition is as the irreversible train of events, the changes which enable us to distinguish yesterday from today, the time now from the time an hour ago. Everything moves headlong into an apparently uncertain future; food is eaten, turned into energy to fuel and repair our bodies, and provide heat to warm us up – higher entropy. Experiences are absorbed by the sensations, using energy, registering memories in our brains, again using energy – higher entropy.

So, could not entropy be described as movement along a time dimension almost as if it were a spatial dimension? How else can movement in the usual sense be described except in terms of the flow of time?

I am suggesting that time does not flow, but that time is a spatial dimension along which entropy flows, and the flow of entropy is manifest in the movement we see around us and every physical process we encounter.

Entropy is the manifestation of the development of the projections from the bosonic energy field from higher six dimensional space into three dimensional space, and the time dimension is necessary in order that these projections can develop using entropy flow.

Without the time dimension and entropy, physical existence would be static and therefore meaningless.

So, I am proposing that time is a spatial dimension, as suggested by P.D.Ouspensky and also hinted at in experiments with dowsing.

Perhaps further proof of this possibility lies in special relativity itself.

This proposes, and it has been proved by experiments with atomic clocks, that time appears to slow down in the presence of a gravitational field such as that produced by the presence of a massive object.

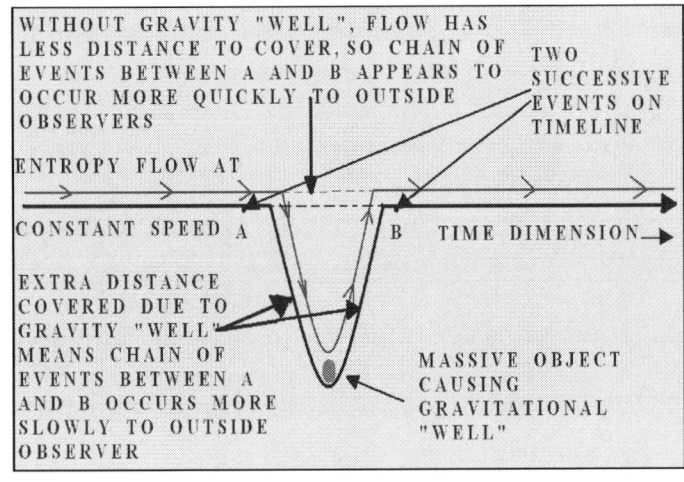

Fig.37. Distortion of Entropy Flow by Gravity.

If we isolate the time dimension from the four dimensional space-time continuum, we can picture this dimension as being distorted by a massive object just as the three spatial dimensions are, as shown in Fig.37.

Now, if this were a spatial dimension in its true sense, objects would accelerate into the gravitational well produced by the massive object, but the time dimension and its associated entropy flow cannot behave in this way.

The flow of entropy maintains a constant speed down into the gravitational well and up the other side. The gravitational well therefore represents extra distance which entropy must cover in the time dimension which would not be there in the absence of the gravitational field. Without the gravitational well, entropy only has to cover the distance represented by the dotted line in Fig.37, between events A and B, whereas in the presence of the massive object, entropy has to cover the extra distance represented by the curvature of the well between events A and B. Therefore, to an objective observer, the time elapsed between event A and event B would seem longer in the presence of gravity. I state "an objective observer" because when you are actually involved in the timeline which is affected by gravity, you are not personally aware of any time dilation taking place.

So, for instance, if event A represents two people of the same age (40) parting company, and event B represents reaching the age of sixty, if one of them were to travel into space where gravitational effects are minimal, his entropy flow (ageing) would follow the dotted line in Fig.37.

If the other one were to stay in the presence of a gravitational field, *his* entropy flow would have to cover the extra distance of the gravitational well, so reaching age sixty, from the point of view of an objective observer, would be a slower process for him, even though he would not be aware of it.

However, he would be aware of it if he then met up again with his now older counterpart, for whom reaching the age sixty was a faster process in the absence of gravity!

According to special relativity, acceleration produces exactly the same effects as gravity.

Well, that is my interpretation of how entropy behaves, but how is it represented in the realms of conventional physics?

This is where our third concept is introduced, that of phase space.

Phase space is the classical physics equivalent of the quantum mechanical Hilbert space. Physics is at the moment divided into two realms, classical physics, which involves Newtonian mechanics and the more recent relativity, (in other words, the macroscopic department) and quantum mechanics (the microscopic department), some aspects of which were covered earlier in this text.

Like Hilbert space, phase space, too, is a mathematical space of enormous dimensionality, each point of which represents the physical state of a (classical) system, the position and momentum information of each individual particle which constitutes the entire system.

To describe the concept of entropy, the phase space is compartmentalised into regions, each region representing the group of physical states which are, on a macroscopic level, indistinguishable from each other.

The smaller the compartment, the lower the entropy of the physical systems represented by that region of phase space. The larger the compartment, the higher the entropy. Mathematically, the entropy is proportional to the logarithm of the compartment volume.

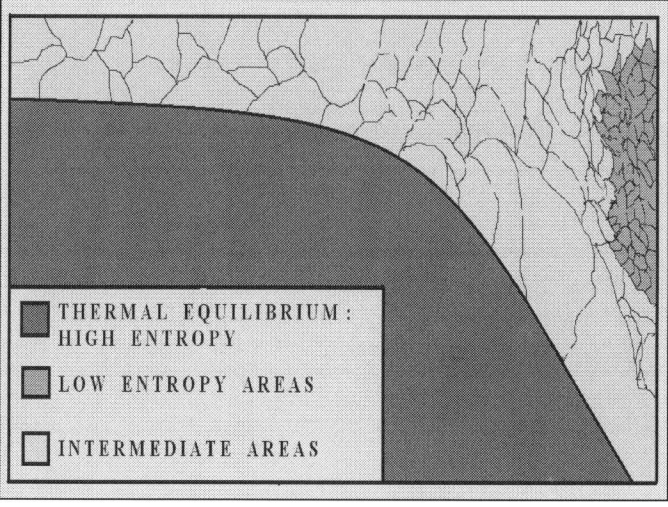

THERMAL EQUILIBRIUM: HIGH ENTROPY

LOW ENTROPY AREAS

INTERMEDIATE AREAS

__Fig.38. Entropy Compartments in Phase Space.__

115

When phase space is compartmentalised in this way to represent entropy, the largest compartment by far is that representing thermal equilibrium, or the highest entropy, when the physical system is in its highest state of disorder possible – when the spring providing the driving force is completely wound down.

Now, to see the Second Law of Thermodynamics in action in a phase space arena, the physical system would start off in the smallest compartment of phase space, representing the state of lowest entropy, and gradually wend its way into compartments of larger volume, representing areas of increasing entropy. These seemingly erratic wanderings are represented by an arrow indicating a vector field. Each subsequent compartment effectively dwarfs the previous compartment by a tremendous factor, until, finally, the physical system finds itself in the compartment which occupies most of the phase space volume – that representing thermal equilibrium, or highest entropy.

See Fig.39 overleaf.

I now intend to develop this train of thought to put a case for the mechanism for the existence of a multitude of realities.

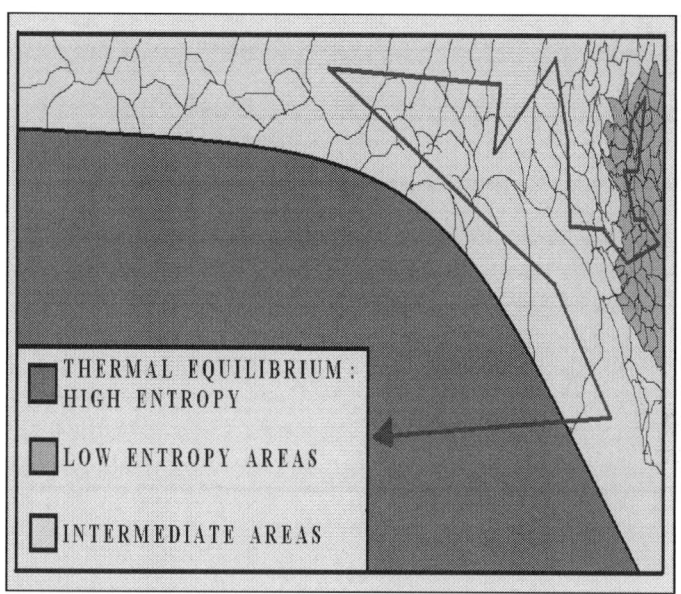

Fig.39. Entropy Increase Represented in Phase Space.

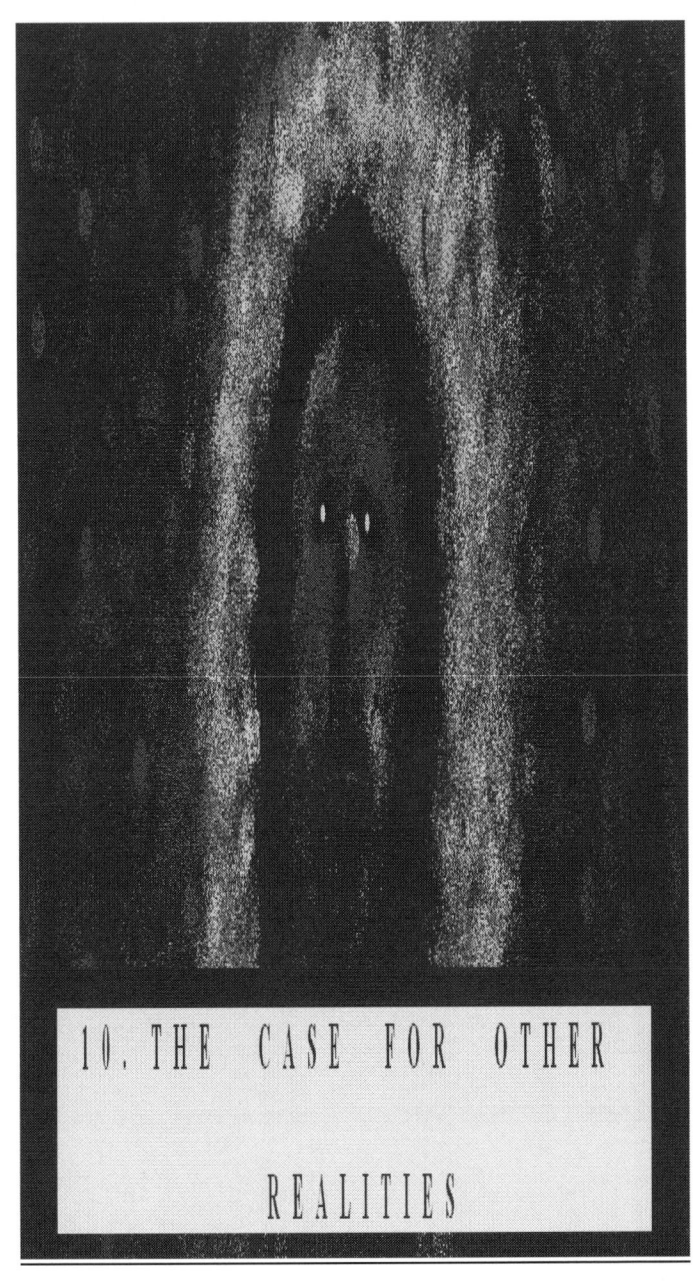

10. THE CASE FOR OTHER

REALITIES

10. The Case for Other Realities.

In the universe we occupy, entropy is always increasing, never decreasing, so from this, we can surmise that when the universe began, in the primordial fireball commonly known as the "Big Bang", a state of lowest entropy, corresponding to the smallest compartments of phase space, was experienced.

Since then, entropy has been increasing and will continue to do so until thermal equilibrium is achieved. If the universe re-collapses, this will be at the "Big Crunch", but in the event this does not happen, and the universe continues to expand, thermal equilibrium is found to exist around black holes.

This is where the Riemann - Christoffel Tensor comes in. I have already briefly explained that this consists of two parts, the Conformal Tensor and the Ricci Tensor. The former measures distortion with volume preservation due to a gravitational field in empty space, whereas the latter measures the overall compression of space-time due to the presence of a massive object.

Now, near a black hole, tidal forces are felt in empty space around it. This is, as I have mentioned, measured by the Conformal Tensor – the Ricci Tensor is zero in empty space. Physicists expect to find that the curvature close to a black hole singularity is completely described by the former. In fact, it tends to infinity. Such behaviour is associated with a singularity of *high* entropy. Such a singularity is known as a *final singularity.*

However, the situation with the "Big Bang" was quite different. In the standard models of the "Big Bang", it is found that any distorting tidal effect due to the Conformal tensor is absent, hence Conf. = 0 here. Instead, any spherical surface present would experience an inward pull due to the tensor Ricci. In fact, Ricci tends to infinity here.

The "Big Bang", therefore, is known as an *initial singularity.*

So, to summarise:

Riemann Christoffel Tensor = Conf. + Ricci.

At initial singularity ("Big Bang"):

Christoffel Tensor = Infinity = Ricci.

At final singularity (Black Hole):

Christoffel Tensor = Infinity = Conf.

Overleaf, I have included two drawings which I hope will help to get across the picture here of the Riemann - Christoffel Tensor as a balancing act between the Conformal and Ricci components.

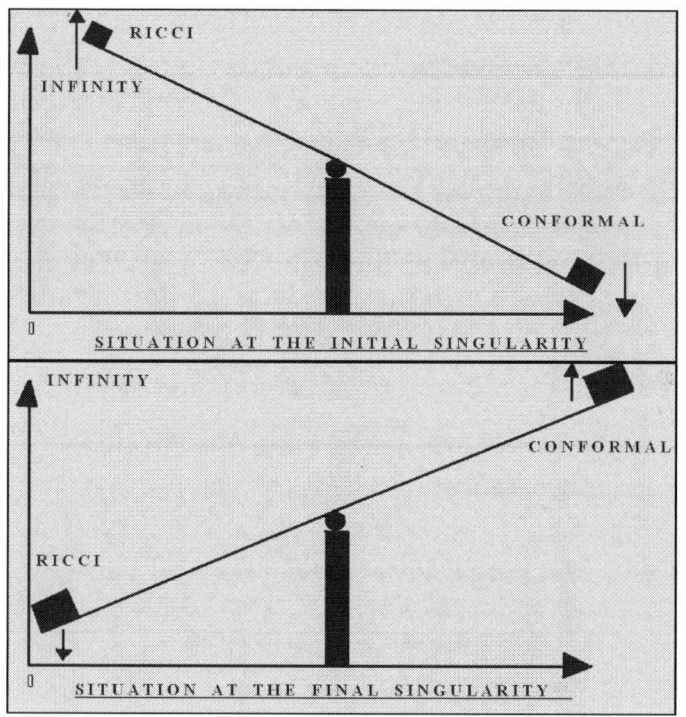

Fig.40 .The Riemann - Christoffel Tensor.

Hence, we have two very different types of singularity here, one which creates everything, the initial singularity, and one which destroys everything, the final singularity. The process of entropy increase marks the path between the two.

But, does a final singularity actually destroy everything? Is that the end?

I would propose a "get out" clause here!

This "get out " clause is as follows, and the same scenario ensues whether the universe recollapses or continues to expand..

Due to the Second Law of Thermodynamics, entropy is forever increasing. As has been mentioned, in phase space, the region of highest entropy is the largest region by far, with regions of lower entropy occupying smaller and smaller compartments. For the conditions commensurate with the "Big Bang", or the initial singularity, entropy must be very low and hence a tiny compartment in phase space is occupied.

The Conformal component of the Riemann Christoffel Tensor is here zero. The universe progresses, modelled by a vector field in phase space (see Fig.39), to entropic compartments of ever increasing volume until when a black hole is formed, the region of highest entropy, thermal equilibrium, is reached. Here, the Conformal component of the Riemann - Christoffel Tensor tends to infinity. This is a final singularity.

However, given long enough, and this is the important part, the vector field *can* find its way to a region of lower entropy, perhaps even the region of lowest entropy, commensurate with an initial singularity, another "Big Bang".

However, the time needed for such an event to occur is stupendously long, but such an event, known as a Poincare recurrence, is not impossible, especially when you consider the distortion of the time dimension relative to us in such an intense gravitational field as that around a black hole.

If the universe continues to expand indefinitely, and the black hole is massive enough that its total evaporation by Hawking radiation does not precede the recurrence, then the formation of an initial singularity within a black hole would seem to be a possibility.

Of course, an initial singularity would seem to be synonymous with the birth of another universe from the black hole, apparently totally unconnected to our own, and from our viewpoint, in our future.

In a constantly expanding infinite universe, infinite numbers of super-massive black holes would give rise to infinite numbers of further initial singularities, hence universes, all of which expand into the three dimensions with which we are familiar in our physical lives. From our viewpoint, these lie in our future.

Resurrecting the uncoiling of a spring analogy:

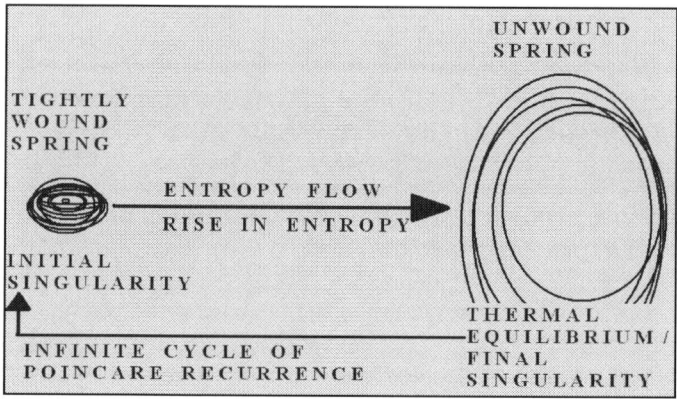

A similar scenario of infinite realities could ensue if the universe recollapses an infinite number of times, forming final singularities.

But why three dimensions in particular? Why do the physical universes not expand into the whole nine dimensional spatial arena, or just into one or two dimensions?

Well, the reason would appear to be that where fermionic, or matter, particles are concerned, which are essential for a physical realm, any more than three dimensions would result in gravitational instabilities which would render such an idea impractical. One can only assume that such instabilities apply even to the quantum level, which would "nip in the bud" any attempt at expansion into more than three dimensions. Thus, the six dimensional realm is reserved purely for the bosonic energy field which includes consciousness.

Of course, one or two dimensions would also be too restrictive.

So, on a physical level, there it is!

But back to the question of these other universes. Is it not feasible that these constitute the arenas for the infinite number of realities which exist? Although, as I have said, from our viewpoint, these extra universes exist in our future, from the standpoint of the six dimensional Calabi-Yau realm, above the temporal plane, all these infinite universes, or realities, exist simultaneously.

So, we can see here that all these new universes created from new initial singularities within black holes actually correspond to the projections from six dimensional higher space into three dimensional space, which then "develop", by the means of entropy flow, along the spatial time dimension. (See Fig.37.)

This simultaneity of existence of multiple realities is also borne out by the wave-function, psi. The peak of the wave-function corresponds to the greatest probability of the particle being found at this point (or of the particle taking this route), but this doesn't rule out the possibility of it being found at other points on the wave-function or taking other routes.

I would suggest that these other points correspond to peaks on psi in other realities – what is highly improbable (but not impossible) in one reality may be the most likely option in another, so viewing in the context of Fig.26, a phase shift effectively takes place.

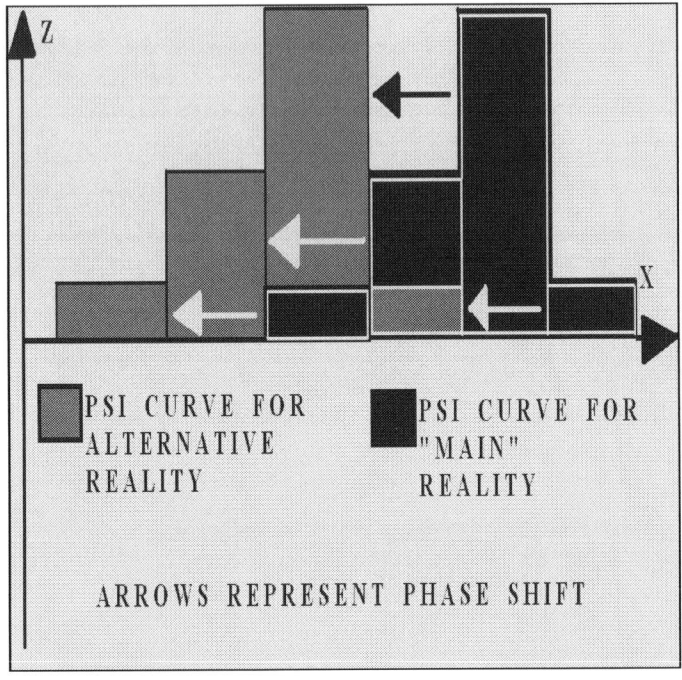

Fig.41 .Non-Zero Probability in One Reality Corresponds to the Highest Probability in Another – Effectively, a Phase Shift.

A quantum super-position, such as is experienced in the two slit experiment, corresponds to momentary existence in multiple realities underlying the one we unconsciously "choose" to experience.

On a macroscopic level, all the quantum super-positions "average out" to give the impression of an objective, solid reality.

But, when the quantum level is reached, the superposition of realities vying for position and interfering with each other (destructively and constructively), becomes more apparent.

Hence, in reality, in the physical realm, we exist in a state of flux between quantum superposition of realities. The macroscopic "averages" give it an objective, solid appearance.

In extreme circumstances, such as in the presence of very strong electromagnetic fields, these "averages" are thrown out of equilibrium and other realities impinge upon the one normally being experienced. Such an occurrence constitutes a general phase shift of the psi curve representing all the quantum states within that system (reality), if only for a short time, until equilibrium is restored, and a more coherent state of flux again exists.

At the end of chapter 7, I mentioned a "striking personal conclusion about the origin O in Fig.36".

As is normally the case with a concept termed "the origin" (!), O represents the starting point of all the infinite number of physical realities in the three dimensional spatial realm. As we have already suggested that all the realities spring from newly-created initial singularities within black holes, O therefore corresponds to all the super-massive black holes which give rise to new initial singularities and hence multiple realities.

O therefore represents the origin of all physical existence.

To be strictly correct, in Fig.36, the flat base of the "fish tank" representing four-dimensional space-time would be better represented as the surface of a sphere, with the reality projections issuing from O and circumnavigating the sphere surface before re-entering O. This is because O effectively represents the end of one reality resulting in the birth of another.

Fig.36 hijacks the concept of Hilbert space to represent the version of reality presented in these pages, but in light of what has just been proposed, let's develop this idea of a sphere.

The sphere would have to be a ten dimensional structure, its surface (the base of the "tank" in Fig.36) representing the three conventional spatial dimensions and the special case of a spatial dimension we call "time"; in other words, four dimensional space-time.

The interior of the sphere (the internal volume of the "tank" in Fig.36) would represent the six dimensional Calabi-Yau realm of the bosonic energy field which incorporates consciousness.

The origin, O, would be at one pole of the sphere. From this point, the state vector representing the bosonic energy field forms a loop within the sphere.

From the same origin, O, emanate the infinite orthogonal projections of the state vector, circumnavigating the surface of the sphere (four-dimensional space-time) before re-entering O.

Now, obviously, a ten dimensional sphere is ridiculously difficult to imagine, let alone draw, so I'm going to exercise the usual sell out scenario and step down the dimensionality to three dimensional sphere represented in the two dimensions of this page. Sorry to disappoint!

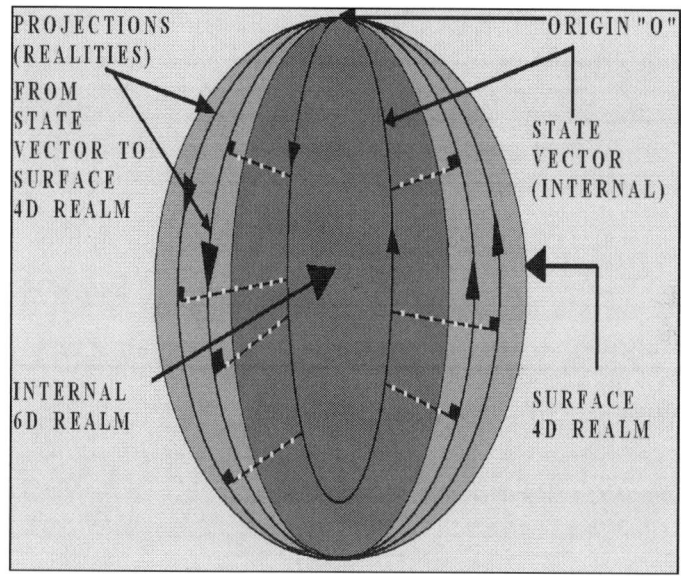

Fig.42. The "Hilbert Sphere".

So, we finally reach the end of this involved section and (yet another) brief summary may be useful at this juncture to hammer the points firmly home before we proceed still further.

A good idea would seem to be to repeat the summary given on P.102 adding on subsequent ideas developed.

What we have so far is a ten dimensional infrastructure, nine dimensions of which consist of space, and one of time, a special case of a spatial dimension itself along which entropy flows.

Six of the spatial dimensions are undetectable from our three dimensional viewpoint, and contain a bosonic energy field, partly consisting of a field of consciousness in the form of a Bose condensate. Infinite combinations of this bosonic energy field, represented in Fig.36 as the state vector, are projected onto the remaining three spatial dimensions and "develop" along the time dimension as a flow of entropy.

The field of consciousness consists of two components, the higher component, which remains embedded in the bosonic energy field in six dimensional space, able to perform Poincare motions to interact with the three dimensional realities in a temporally unrelated fashion, and a lower component, which can move in tandem along the time dimension, experiencing the multiple projections of the bosonic energy field as realities in three dimensional space.

When "in phase" with a particular projection, a transform to fermionic matter occurs (it detects the energy field as matter), and this is described as a "lifetime".

"Phase shifts" can sometimes be experienced, usually in the presence of strong energy fields, and this can sometimes result in the impingement of one reality onto another, a brief merging of projections.

One particular facet of the lower consciousness is only aware of one lifetime at a time, although its higher component is simultaneously aware of them all, being detached from the time dimension.

This is the means by which people experience such phenomena as precognition and retro-cognition, temporary super- awareness instigated by interaction with the higher consciousness.

Upon physical death, reintegration with the higher consciousness occurs in most cases, but occasionally, total reintegration does not occur and the lower consciousness remains in the three dimensional realm as a disembodied Bose condensate which has limited physical interaction with the fermionic world it subconsciously chooses to inhabit, i.e. a ghost.

Another similar phenomenon is astral travelling, whereby the lower component of the Bose condensate wanders the three dimensional realm it inhabits free of the physical body during sleep or unconsciousness, although a return to the physical body(!) is usually experienced, and, at this stage, desired!

All infinite realities occur in the same three dimensional space arena simultaneously, but they originate from one origin, "O", in Fig.36.

This origin represents all the newly created universes from initial singularities which eventually form within super-massive black holes, by means of Poincare recurrences, in

previous universes, giving scope to the infinite number of realities experienced.

Fig.36 could be better represented as a ten-dimensional sphere, with the origin at one pole, the state vector forming an internal loop starting and finishing at the origin, and the infinite projections of this state vector circumnavigating the surface of the sphere which represents four- dimensional space-time.

The interior of the sphere would represent the remaining six dimensional realm containing consciousness and the bosonic energy field.

Each projection onto its surface would stem from the origin, circumnavigating the sphere back to the origin, then circumnavigate via a different trajectory along the surface back to the origin and so forth.

This circumnavigation back to the origin and round again and again (infinitely) through the origin would represent the constant formation of infinite realities by means of initial singularities occurring within black holes.

But now, the question remains, perhaps the most important question of all: why?

What does this all mean?

Why would it be structured like this?

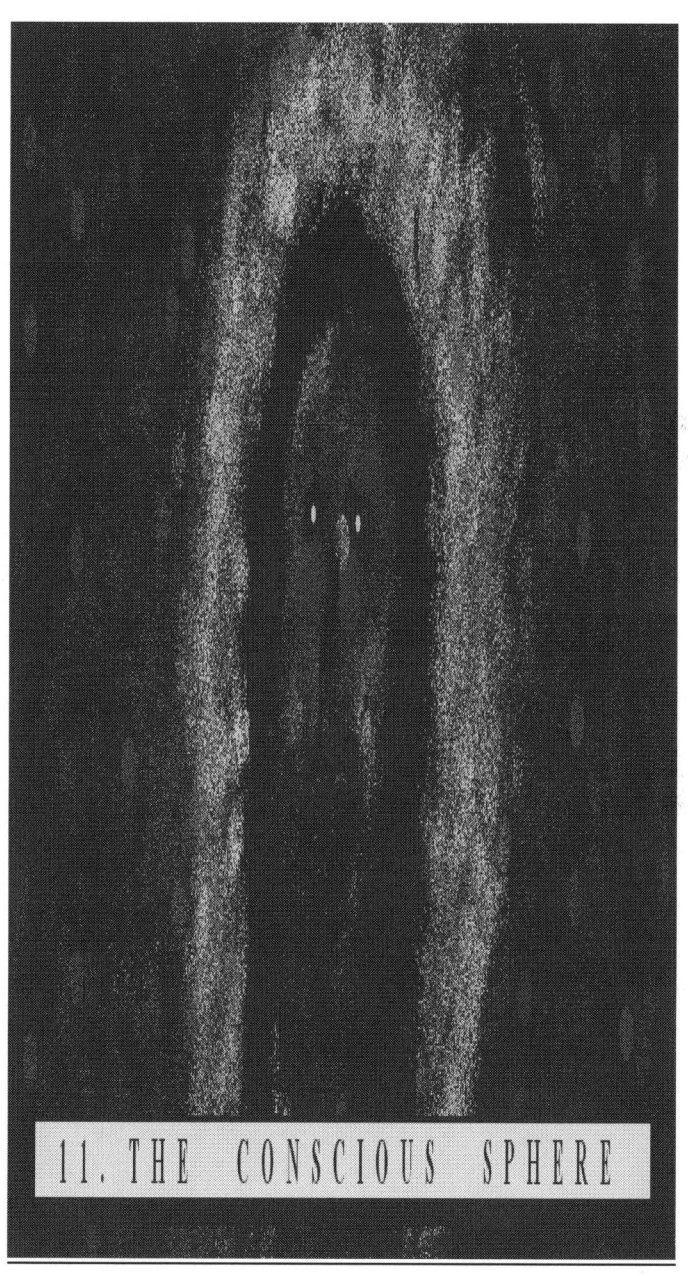

11. THE CONSCIOUS SPHERE

11 . The Conscious Sphere.

I wish now to resurrect the idea of our consciousness as a physical ground state known as a Bose condensate, which as the reader will recall is a highly coherent steady state which unifies all our disparate physical experiences and gives consciousness its holistic nature.

Recall the basic quantum coherence suggested by Herbert Frohlich back on P.40. If we wind the evolutionary clock back to the beginning of life itself, such basic quantum coherence would surely be seen, but would this have an ultimate goal in mind?

In this final chapter, I intend to propose that it would, and attempt to suggest a physical idea which would enable this to take place.

We're all reasonably familiar with the concept of evolution, but why would evolution involve an increasing complexity within physical organisms when a simple life form can get by quite well as it is?

On the surface, the answer to me seems quite obvious! Think about it! Could a simple life form support the elaborate consciousness – the sense of self – which we find, for instance, in a human being? I would contend, and no doubt anyone would have to agree, that the answer is a resounding "No", and I would also contend that what we are at the moment is only a stepping stone in our evolution to even greater physical complexity, supporting even greater quantum coherence and hence more sophisticated consciousness.

As we have already postulated that consciousness is bosonic in nature, perhaps it can also be said that a proto-consciousness arises when two bosons overlap their identity.

At this point, I will (again!) recap on the idea of what a boson is to save you flicking through the pages in case you've forgotten!

Bosons consist of all the virtual particles which constitute the forces which occur on a subatomic level, such as gluons, which bind the nuclei of atoms together, and constitute the strong nuclear force; the gauge bosons, which constitute the weak nuclear force which governs radioactive decay; photons, which carry the electromagnetic force, and finally, gravitons, which transmit the gravitational force.

These virtual particles have an affinity to overlapping their identities and merging as one – this idea is particularly important.

The other type are the fermions, which are the matter particles, such as protons, neutrons and electrons which would prefer to be "lone groovers" and do not possess a natural affinity to merging their identity with the "whole".

The efforts of the bosons force them together to constitute a reality in the physical sense.

Speculation in scientific circles would have it that consciousness initiates state vector collapse, but it is also a contention that this occurs when two bosons "entangle".

If consciousness is indeed bosonic, then the first statement would appear to be true.

In other words, bosonic interaction itself automatically "chooses" which reality projection to opt for at a given point on the time dimension, even at such an elementary level as this.

This process of entanglement is effectively irreversible in the physical realm, so the process of bosonic interaction can only go forward into increasing complexity.

As well as constituting the building blocks of consciousness, they are the mortar which binds the fermionic bricks. Bosons need to bind fermions together to build sufficiently complex structures to house their own more complex coherence, hence the physical realities as we know them.

Everything is thought to originate from what physicists call the quantum vacuum, a potential field from which everything (bosonic and fermionic) arises.

Relating this to string theory, perhaps the quantum vacuum is synonymous with the six dimensional Calabi-Yau spaces which are necessary for sufficient string (or membrane) oscillation to give rise to the panoply of elementary particles which exist.

Very interestingly, from the point of view of this book, some physicists are proposing that one of the fields in the quantum vacuum is a Bose condensate, which you will recall comprises the ground state required for consciousness.

This mirrors rather closely what is being proposed here: that the higher consciousness exists in the Calabi-Yau realm.

Some daring souls even posit the idea that the vacuum itself is conscious, and furthermore, that it has an ultimate goal towards ever increasing complexity and sophistication of consciousness itself.

This is achieved through physical experiences gathered through all lifetimes in the physical realm.

Recall that the Bose condensate which constitutes our consciousness in the physical realm can be referred to as the lower consciousness, but it has a higher component whose realm is above the dimension of time in the six dimensional Calabi-Yau realm, what physicists would prefer to call the quantum vacuum, an ocean of possibilities.

I stated earlier in the text that a restriction on the higher consciousness to exist in isolation would be a fallacy:

"Is it possible that interconnectedness exists between our personal higher consciousness and everyone else's, living or dead.....?

If such interconnectedness does indeed exist, we open up to an idea not just of unity within a particular consciousness, but unity of all consciousness; super-consciousness, in effect."

This idea has been touched upon by Rupert Sheldrake's absorbing idea of "morphic resonance", which postulates a "morphic field" which an entire species tunes into and adapts accordingly.

Ideas are "in the air", a concept known as "zeitgeist", and if a consciousness resonates at the appropriate frequency, it will be receptive to them.

A similar theme of unity was suggested in 1919 by biologist Paul Kammerer in his Law of Seriality, which suggests a grouping of the phenomena we call coincidences.

He speculated that all events were connected by waves of Seriality, unknown unifying forces which are so profoundly interlinked that we merely detect the superficial structure as coincidences.

Perhaps the connecting force in question is our unified, collective higher consciousness.

Einstein himself, on reviewing Kammerer's work, said that the idea of Seriality was "interesting and by no means absurd". In fact, this may have been a veiled insult, as Einstein also said that the more absurd an idea was, the more likely it was to be actually true!

Arthur Schopenhauer, on the subject of coincidences, also hinted at an underlying unity:

"Coincidences are not just motivated by physical causality, but a subjective connection to the environment. They (coincidences) were important as they were tailor-made to fit individuals and were only relevant on a personal level."

Could this be an intuitive sense on the part of the philosopher of the interaction of the higher consciousness, bosonic in nature, on the physical environment, fermionic in nature, pertaining to its corresponding lower consciousness to directly affect its life path to take the desired route?

This also touches upon the idea that consciousness can have a direct influence (usually subconsciously) on the apparently external environment.

Carl Gustav Jung later developed the idea of synchronicity along these lines, a formal definition being:

"The coincidence in time of two or more causally- unrelated events which have the same meaning."

Even as far back as the 5th Century B.C., a similar idea of underlying unity was expressed by Hippocrates:

"There is one common flow, one common breathing, all things are in sympathy. The whole organism, and each one of its parts, is working in conjunction for the same purpose. The great principle extends to the extremest part, and from the extremest part, it returns to the great principle, to the one nature being and not being."

University of London physicist David Bohm suggested that the universe is a hologram, every part containing the whole order. He believed this was projected from higher dimensions, each level containing sentience.

Does this sound in any way familiar?

So, an underlying unity appears to be a theme running through the whole structure, combined with a tendency towards ever increasing physical complexity which goes hand in hand with ever increasing complexity of consciousness through quantum coherence.

Recall Fig.16, which I have used to imply that consciousness is able to transcend the frame of reference in which the speed of light restriction applies.

In this way, it is able to manipulate, as easily as we in the physical manipulate three dimensions, the space-time continuum in such a way that it can impinge at any time and any place in the projected realities instantaneously and simultaneously in its higher form.

If our higher self can impart thoughts and ideas in this way, interconnectedness with other higher selves in six dimensional space could enrich this process to produce morphic resonance, and could also, by the same process, affect physical events, however trivial, meaningful to the lower selves concerned, with the aim of enriching their physical experience and giving it direction.

This interconnectedness between higher selves could explain time-slips, or retro-cognition, and perhaps precognition: the projection of vivid conscious experiences between lower selves via their higher counterparts across the spatial time dimension.

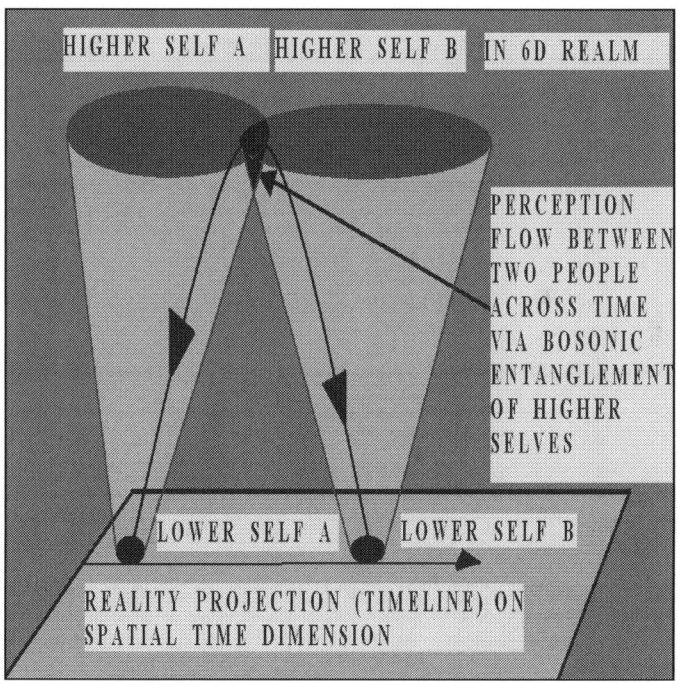

HIGHER SELF A   HIGHER SELF B   IN 6D REALM

PERCEPTION FLOW BETWEEN TWO PEOPLE ACROSS TIME VIA BOSONIC ENTANGLEMENT OF HIGHER SELVES

LOWER SELF A   LOWER SELF B

REALITY PROJECTION (TIMELINE) ON SPATIAL TIME DIMENSION

Fig.43. The Flow of Temporally-Separated Perceptions Via Higher Unification.

This interconnectedness arises through the natural affinity of bosons to overlap their identity. As consciousness is bosonic in nature, this is a natural occurrence.

We all occasionally have the feeling of "déjà vu", when a short sequence of events occurs which seems strangely familiar.

This could be explained in a similar way to that described in Fig.43, except the flow of perceptions is carried through a single higher consciousness.

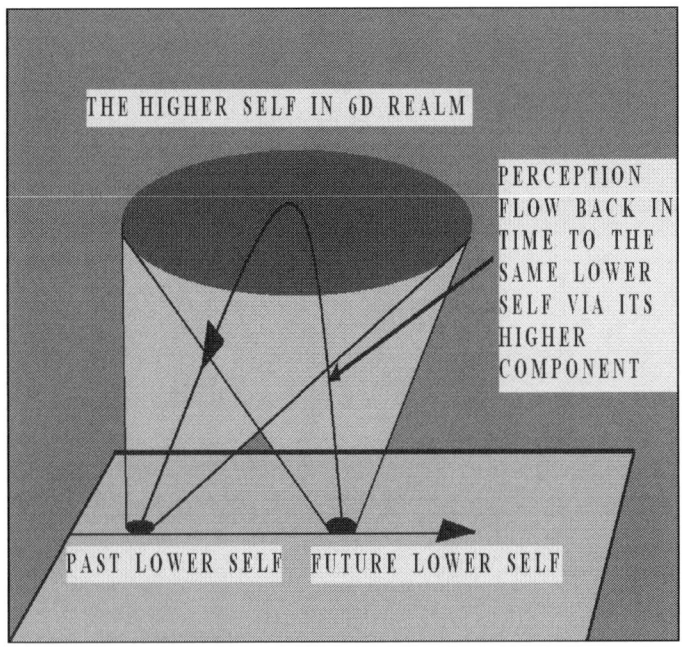

Fig.44. The Flow of Temporally –Separated Perceptions Via One Higher Consciousness.

You may have noticed that the major difference between Figs.43 and 44 is that two distinct but unified higher selves are involved in retro-cognition and precognition, as these phenomena can, and usually do, involve perceptions from separate physical beings, whereas déjà vu normally involves perceptions by the same person, hence just the single higher consciousness in Fig.44.

Thus, so far, we have the idea that creation itself not only seems to possess some kind of underlying unity, which we in the physical sense find difficult to either believe or discern, but also some kind of direction towards increasing complexity, giving rise in the process to more complex realms of consciousness.

But why would this be so?

For the next step of this missive, I intend to introduce the idea of backward causation, or retro-causation, as it is sometimes labelled.

This is a fairly complex idea, but in terms of the ideas in these pages, perhaps not quite as complex as it may seem. More counter-intuitive, I think!

In the physical, temporal plane in which we exist, cause always precedes effect, but the idea of retro-causation implies that although this is the case, cause and effect need not be temporally in order.

Before you begin to think I perhaps should be sectioned under the Mental Health Act, let me explain!

In other words, if you can rise above the spatial dimension of time as postulated within this text, a cause which is in the future on the temporal plane can have an effect which is temporally speaking in the past!

Imagine the temporal plane as a glass tabletop pushed against the wall. The nearer the wall you get on the tabletop, the further in the future you are.

Now, a picture falls off the wall and impacts on the table directly against the wall (in the future), but a large crack gradually appears and works its way along the tabletop away from the wall (into the past).

Admittedly, this is a very rough analogy (!), but I hope you get the general picture that an event in the future on the temporal plane can have an impact on events in the past, even though we don't realise it when we are in the physical.

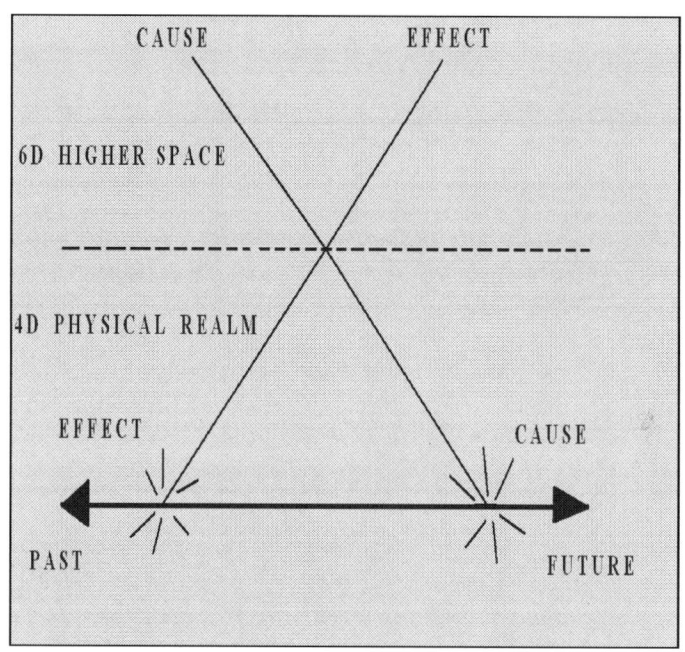

Fig.45. The Essence of Retro-causation.

By operating in the six dimensional higher space, the entire physical temporal plane is at your disposal and you can potentially, in tandem with other aspects of higher consciousness within this realm, influence events and trains of thought at any point in the space-time continuum, which contains infinite physical realities, in order to achieve the desired effect on the upper right of Fig.45.

Thus, you, as a higher dimensional being, can instigate an event on the lower right of Fig.45 which repurcusses backwards through time to cause the effect on the lower left of

145

Fig.45, which is the desired ultimate effect on the top right.

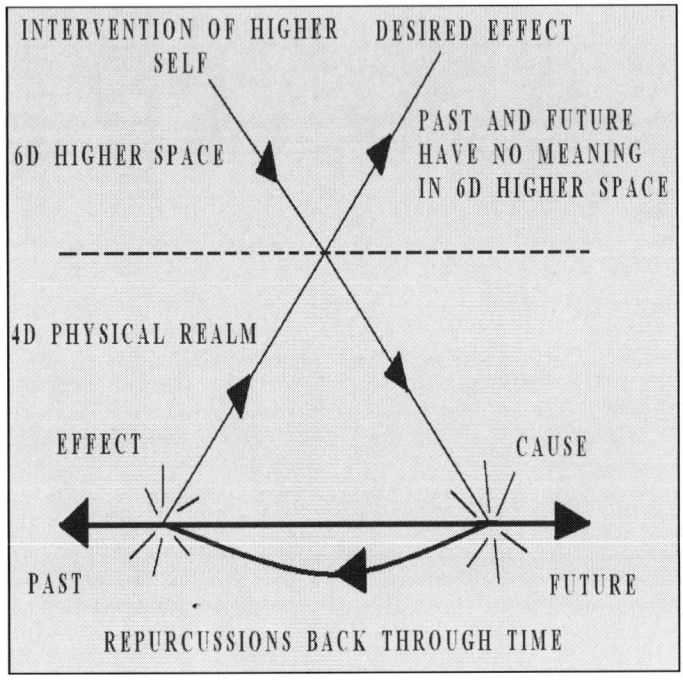

INTERVENTION OF HIGHER SELF   DESIRED EFFECT

6D HIGHER SPACE

PAST AND FUTURE HAVE NO MEANING IN 6D HIGHER SPACE

4D PHYSICAL REALM

EFFECT   CAUSE

PAST   FUTURE

REPURCUSSIONS BACK THROUGH TIME

Fig.46. Retro-causation and Intervention of Higher Consciousness.

When you think about it, this can have rather strange implications.

On the top left of Fig.46, let's say there are two (for the sake of simplicity!) higher selves overlapping their identities as previously described. However, their union is not quite complete, as one of the partnership lacks the total depth of the other.

146

On the physical plane, they were father and son, and they both agree, in the higher dimension, that the early death of one of them on the physical plane would help the spiritual development of the surviving one, as this event would instigate a drastic change of life style which would be ultimately beneficial. This decision is taken at the top left of Fig.46.

In order for the death of one of the pair to occur, an event is instigated at the bottom right of Fig.46, which requires, in order for it to occur, a built in series of events leading up to it within the reality projection concerned. This "built in" series of events are the repurcussions which travel backwards through time but which we on the physical plane detect as normal cause and effect in normal sequence.

The inevitable result of one of these repurcussions is the death of either father or son at the bottom left of Fig.46, the resulting effect being, at the top right, the increased empathy experienced by the higher pair as a direct result of the increased spiritual development of the surviving physical being during his lifetime due to the change in lifestyle brought on by the early death of his loved one!!

This is the essence, if anything, of this entire work – that time and the physical plane as we know it are but the tip of the proverbial iceberg!

(It is possible to speculate here about the relationship between the human brain and the Bose condensate – which sustains which? The usual view would be that the brain supports the coherent condensate which gives rise to our consciousness, but could it not be possible that the Bose-Einstein condensate forms a template for the brain outside of our temporal realm which the physical realm then strives to fulfil?)

In fact, the above example could possibly explain why deceased loved ones don't (often!) come back to reassure us of life after death or even comfort us. It's simply because, on the six dimensional plane, we're with them already! A slight intervention every now and then on the physical plane at times of great stress generally suffices, and this is probably "inserted" into the life experience by mutual agreement of the aspects of higher consciousness directly involved.

However, here we find ourselves in somewhat of a contradictory situation, at least at first glance. Why would the higher consciousness wish to instigate changes in a particular reality in order to achieve certain desired effects when infinitesimal realities already exist, as stated earlier? Surely a reality tailor-made to suit the course of events required would already exist?

Well, I would argue that the infinite realities which already exist do so as a direct result of the intervention of higher consciousness on the physical plane – realities are created, complete with their entire self-consistent histories, to suit the physical experiences required of the lower selves by their higher counterparts. So, the situation described in Fig.46 would result in the creation of an entirely new reality projection where the early death of the father resulted in a more profound physical experience for the lower self concerned, which in turn results, from the aspect of six dimensional higher space, in the immediate increased spiritual depth of one of the higher entities overlapping their identity with the other. I wish to stress that in higher space, removed from the constraints of the temporal plane, the effect brought about by the creation of this new reality is absolutely immediate – no sooner is the reality created than the spiritual effect on the unified higher consciousness is enacted. It is an ongoing process, yielding immediate results.

So, retro-causation, in this context, is the built-in history of a newly-created reality leading up to the key event(s) for which that reality was created.

But, retro-causation has a much more profound implication than this.

In view of what has just been said, could not each such act resulting in the increased complexity of unified higher selves in the six dimensional higher space eventually result in the formation of a highly complex, highly coherent and therefore omniscient amalgamation of higher consciousness – a super-consciousness, in effect?

Ultimately, could such a spiritual superpower influence events on the physical plane in such a way that the ever increasing complexity of physical life we have just discussed takes place? Do you now perceive a curiously self-sustaining cyclical process emerging?

We have already touched upon the idea that increasing physical complexity gives rise to more complex consciousness, eventually resulting in a super-complex consciousness. *But, this super-consciousness initiates the process of increasing complexity in the physical realms by retro-causation!*

As each of us is an aspect of this super-consciousness, by token of the higher/lower partnership, in tandem with others' higher selves and therefore their lower selves too, each individual consciousness has its part to play in the development towards the omniscient consciousness of which we are *already* a part.

This is the reason for our physical existences, in which we acquire knowledge and form relationships with others.

It would be difficult for a totally coherent super-consciousness to form if each of its aspects acted in isolation.

Spiritualists would perhaps refer to this process of development through physical experience "soul growth". A succinct representation is shown in Fig.47.

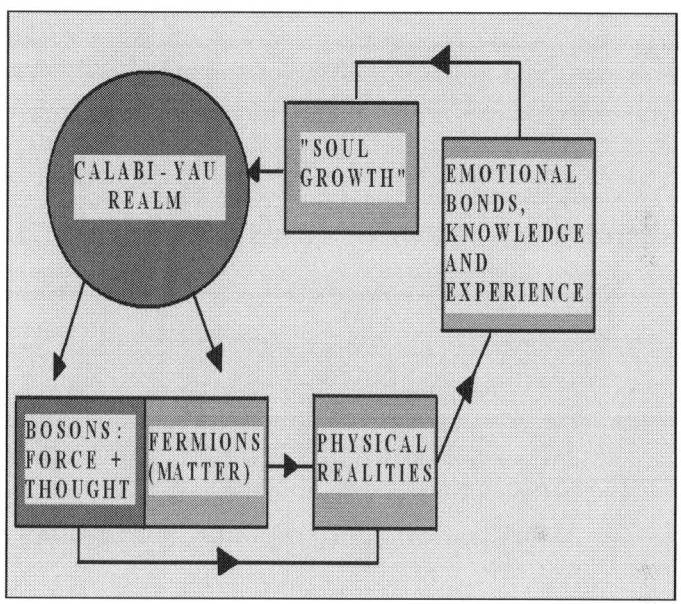

Fig.47. The Cyclical Nature of "Soul Growth".

In this way, by a universal process of retro-causation, we are all in the process of becoming what we already are in the first place! Our physical existences are "tailored" to promote "soul growth" and eventual fusion into the super-consciousness of which we are already a part. If the eventual super-consciousness did not exist, from our point of

151

view in our distant future, then our entire existence would be meaningless and without direction. There would be no need for the increasing complexity of life-forms to produce the emergent phenomenon of consciousness – to what end?

It can almost be crudely envisaged as a strange suction process, whereby the super-consciousness is drawing everything towards it to sustain itself. Without this sustenance, it would shrivel and die. Likewise, without the super-consciousness, the currents in the medium in which it exists would cease and there would be no sense of directional flow within the medium itself.

Admittedly, this is a strange idea to try to impart, transcending as it does our ideas of space and time and cause and effect.

However, to understand this, we must transcend the physical realms which we only fleetingly inhabit on our unshakeable journey towards unity within the omniscient super-consciousness which is at the very heart of the meaning to our existence, and represents our ultimate destiny.

If there is an "easy" way to picture this process, I have visualised the entire development as a seven stage cyclical process as shown in the final illustration of this text, romantically named "Fig.48" to be found on P.154.

A Very Short Conclusion.

So, we reach the end of our extremely involved journey! I hope that you've found the reading of these pages as rewarding as I have found it writing them.

True....it's not "War and Peace". To be honest, it was never intended to be. I feel that making the book unnecessarily long would have been a pointless exercise filled with far too much "waffle" (let's face it, some of you may feel this as it is!), but I've tried to keep the salient points as succinct as possible without wandering too far from the subject at hand.

I also hope that the subject matter was not totally unfathomable; I've endeavoured to keep it as simple as possible (!).

The whole spirit of this work can be summed up thus:

As innumerable philosophers have hinted at through the ages, death is not to be feared as the end of your personal experience.

On the contrary, it is the start of the next stage of your great journey towards ultimate enlightenment.

I'll leave you with a quote from Schopenhauer's "Essay on Death":

"Death is not final, merely a transition to another impersonal kind of existence, a reunion with a state of cosmic one-ness."

1 ← HIGHLY COHERENT SUPERCONSCIOUSNESS

STAGE 7 — SOUL GROWTH THROUGH LIFE EXPERIENCE

STAGE 6 — CREATION OF UNIVERSES / REALITIES IN BLACK HOLES

STAGE 5 — INCREASING COHERENCE / COMPLEXITY

STAGE 4 — COMBINE

STAGE 3 — BOSONS : FORCE AND CONSCIOUSNESS | FERMIONS: MATTER

STAGE 2 — BIG BANG : DIVISION INTO 6D CALABI - YAU SPACE | AND 4D REALM

154

Recommended Reading.

Synchronicity – The Promise of Coincidence
Deike Begg.

The Elegant Universe
Brian Greene.

A Brief History of Time
Stephen Hawking.

Life After Life
Dr. Raymond Moody.

Tertium Organum
P.D. Ouspensky.

Is There Life After Death?
Anthony Peake.

The Emperor's New Mind
Roger Penrose.

Strange But True
Colin, Damon and Rowan Wilson.

The Quantum Self
Danah Zohar and Dr. Ian Marshall.

Index.

157

Final Acknowledgments.

I would like to express my eternal gratitude to my wife, Gillian, without whom I would still be "out on the lash" and would never have thought of all this in the first place!!
Also, to my daughter, Alex, who guided me through the pitfalls and vagaries of Microsoft Word.

The adaptations of diagrams from "The Emperor's New Mind" by Roger Penrose were used by kind permission of Oxford University Press. www.oup.co.uk

The image of the Calabi – Yau manifold is to be found in Wikipedia (as I found it impossible to draw!).
The original author is listed as "jbourjai".
The source file is:

http://en.wikipedia.org/wiki/File:Calabi_yau.jpg #file

The light cone diagrams were derived from one in Wikipedia.
The author is listed as K.Aainsqatsi.
The source file is:

http://en.wikipedia.org/wiki/Image:World_line.png

The diagrams of the Two Slit Experiment were derived from ones in Wikipedia. For the first one: The author is listed as: en:User:Lacatosias,User:Stannered. The source file is:

http://en.wikipedia.org/wiki/File:Ebohr1.svg

For the second one: The author is listed as Dr.Tanamura. The source file is:

http://en.wikipedia.org/wiki/File:Double-slit_experiment_results_Tanamura_2.jpg

The information on Quantum Consciousness was derived from a file in Wikipedia. The source file is:

http://en.wikipedia.org/wiki/Quantum_mind

All the items derived from Wikipedia articles is available under the

GNU FREE DOCUMENTATION LICENSE

The link to this is:

http://en.wikipedia.org/wiki/Wikipedia:Text_of_the_GNU_Free_Documentation_License

163

Finally, I would like to thank you for buying this book and hope you have enjoyed it as much as I have enjoyed writing it. It makes all the hard work worthwhile!

Also, don't forget to drop me a line on my Blog:

http://kaluzaconcept.com/

or on my Squidoo lens:

http://www.squidoo.com/kaluzaconcept

Any comments and contributions from yourselves would be most welcome....or just drop in for a chat!!

Printed in Great Britain
by Amazon

55551726R00095